Anecdotes & Analysis

from Nicaragua

Rice & Beans & Hope
by Thomas Montgomery-Fate

Models of Church in Nicaragua
by Rafael Aragón & José María Vigil

Introduction by
Robert McAfee Brown

Anecdotes & Analysis

from Nicaragua

Rice & Beans & Hope
by Thomas Montgomery-Fate

Models of Church in Nicaragua
by Rafael Aragón & José María Vigil

Introduction by
Robert McAfee Brown

© 1988 New York CIRCUS Publications, Inc., New York, NY   ISBN 0-936123-04-4

BX
1442.2
.A52
1988

CONTENTS

Prologue *VII*
Introduction by Robert McAfee Brown *IX*

RICE AND BEANS AND HOPE
Thomas Montgomery-Fate

On Saving the World	3
Carlos	4
Navidad	7
Going for Water	13
On Time	19
On Time in Managua	23
Safe At Home	28
Communion	37
Taking Poneloya	44
Selling Pop	51
Danny	58
Christmas	62

MODELS OF CHURCH IN NICARAGUA
Rafael Aragon & Jose Maria Vigil

Three Models of Church in Nicaragua	69
Three Models of the Church	71
The Three Models in Nicaragua	83
Ecclesial Base Communities and The Post-Revolutionary Ecclesiological Model	87

PROLOGUE

"But the War is Over...Isn't It ?

"But the war is over, isn't it? The contras have been defeated. There are the Peace Accords. Why are you publishing a book on Nicaragua now?"

Yes, that phase of U.S. aggression against Nicaragua does appear to be winding down. The Reagan administration's overt military aggression through a second surrogate force - the contras - has failed. Recent reports from the battlefields of Nicaragua indicate that contra soldiers and Sandinistas are meeting and sharing their desires for peace. The morale of the contras has been broken; the stranglehold policy of the Reagan administration has failed. The winds for peace, of a cease-fire, are in the air.

So why publish a book on Nicaragua now? The war may be over, but there is no guarantee that U.S. aggression has come to an end. There is no guarantee that the failure of the contras means a lifting of the economic blockade, a U.S. commitment to fulfilling the Peace Accords or official U.S. recognition of the Nicaraguan government. For example, bi-partisan aid for the rehabilitation of children who have been victims of the war is, by U.S. law, forbidden to pass through institutions of the Nicaraguan government. In a country where the entire health care system is a government project, the aid package appears doomed to failure, in practice breaking the spirit of the Peace Accords and blowing against the winds of peace that are moving in the region.

New York CIRCUS Publications has committed itself to making Anecdotes and Analysis coming from Nicaragua available in English during this next period so that North American Christians and others interested in the Nicaraguan experience can begin to become aware of emerging U.S. policy. New York CIRCUS Publications believes that Nicaragua was more than a "justice issue" under the Reagan administration. We believe that the process for self-determination begun by the Nicaraguan people will need to be monitored continually as a new U.S. foreign policy is carved for the region - one which many feel will continue aggression against Nicaragua in one form or another.

Tom Montgomery-Fate's Anecdotes take us close to the subjects of the Nicaraguan Revolution: the people themselves. Rafael Aragon's Analysis gives us a framework for understanding the tendencies within the institutional church in Nicaragua. The analysis provides the framework for understanding the ideological struggle within one institution - the church - as Nicaragua enters a new period in its history.

New York CIRCUS Publications releases RICE AND BEANS AND HOPE: ANECDOTES AND ANALYSIS FROM NICARAGUA as a part of its efforts to introduce North American Christians to the present Nicaraguan reality. This piece complements our larger project of publishing a new bi-monthly magazine, AMANECER, the English edition of the official magazine of the Antonio Valdivieso Ecumenical Center in Managua.

Yes, the war is over. The Nicaraguan process goes on, as will efforts within U.S. foreign policy mechanisms to stop it. During the next few years ANECDOTES AND ANALYSIS will be an important reference for North Americans who continue to keep themselves informed about events and people in Nicaragua. ANECDOTES AND ANALYSIS will be important as we seek to build our framework for understanding the next U.S. foreign policy initiatives in Central America.

New York CIRCUS Publications, Inc.
New York, New York
June, 1988

INTRODUCTION

Analysis and anecdotes...

That's a pretty good combination for finding out about what is going on in the world, particularly in places that are initially strange to us. Analysis alone can be impersonal; anecdotes alone can be fuzzy. We really need both, and that is what this book provides.

Despite its centrality in the news for the last seven or eight years, Nicaragua is still "strange" to most of us. We have read a lot, we have heard news reports galore, and many of us have taken sides in the interminable debates over "arms to the contras," and whether Nicaragua is what is perjoratively called a "Marxist-Leninist dictatorship" or the scene of a modern revolution that just might succeed in establishing justice, if the Reagan administration would leave it alone.

Part of the reason Nicaragua remains strange is that so many of the people who make pronouncements about it either haven't been there (like President Reagan) or rely for their information on people who view everything in Nicaragua from ideologically entrenched perspectives (like President Reagan's reliance on Elliott Abrams to give him the "truth" about Nicaragua).

At no point, perhaps, do we receive more conflicting reports about Nicaragua than in the area of what is happening in the churches. To the hard-liners, the church in Nicaragua is under constant attack by atheist politicians, barely surviving, and crippled by "leftist" defections within the ranks of its priests. To those, on the other hand, who try to see the church in Nicaragua in relation to the whole Latin

American scene – with its stress on the "theology of liberation" and base communities – the Nicaraguan church is a tremendously important example of trying to relate an ageless gospel to an endlessly changing world, and being for once on the side of social change rather than against it.

Rafael Aragon and Jose Maria Vigil's analysis of the church situation can help to guide us through this tangle. As he indicates, at least by implication, traditional "models" of the church – or even new models conceived within a traditional framework – don't quite fit the Nicaraguan scene, and after laying them out in principle he shows how Nicaraguan realities modify the very preconceptions we bring to ecclesiological discussion. This may be the most important contribution of his analysis, since it serves as a clear reminder not to bring preconceptions to the Nicaraguan scene and "fit" the evidence to support them. Something new is in the wind, and Nicaraguans are at the forefront of those being propelled by the new and creative currents.

It is a sense of the new and creative currents that we discern in Tom Montgomery-Fate's anecdotes, the vignettes, the episodes. They do not bear much writing about since the only way, finally, to do justice to a story is to read it, rather than analyzing it. If the author had wanted to evoke analysis he would have written an analytic piece about all the wonderful characters he shares with us in his verbal portraits. So the advice here is ancient Christian advice: tolle, lege, take up and read.

What emerges most clearly from these anecdotes is that Nicaraguans are people, not exemplifications of an ideology or a party-line political posture. They ache, they eat (when they can), they fight (when they must), they worship, they cry, they are uncommonly friendly to gringos whose country has been trying to destroy their country, and they would like nothing better than for our government to get off their backs and let them ache, eat, fight, worship, cry and be friendly on their own volition and on their own terms.

This is the side of Nicaragua we don't hear about from the White House or on the six o'clock news.

Thanks to Tom Montgomery-Fate for introducing us to all his friends. Thanks to Rafael Aragon and Jose Maria Vigil for presenting us with a challenging analysis.

Robert McAfee Brown
Professor Emeritus of Theology and Ethics
Pacific School of Religion
Berkeley, California
May, 1988

Rice & Beans & Hope

by Thomas Montgomery-Fate

ON SAVING THE WORLD

Mr. Johnson, my sixth grade social studies teacher, told us that the Third World was "underdeveloped," places like Africa and India. We spent several warm sleepy afternoons watching movies about these places; lots of dark-skinned people that wore robes and had babies hanging on them. It was always hot and they lived in little huts. There were a lot of flies and not enough to eat. But the U.S. was sending them tractors and seeds and engineers and doctors to "help them to help themselves." That always made us feel better.

The summer of that same year, in Sunday School, we pasted these little blue and white maps of the world on some Pepsi cans. Around the top of the can we attached stickers that said "Save the Children." We were supposed to take these little banks home and keep them in a place where we'd see them a lot, to remind us that everyone didn't have enough food or clothes or clean water. Since my Dad was a minister we had to talk about it all the time. Like at dinner my Mom would always ask if I put in my dime that day.

It seemed like everyone was trying to save the children or the world or something back then. But I was never quite sure which it was or why. My older brothers were marching on Washington and burning their draft cards, while others were parachuting out of helicopters onto rice fields and spraying napalm. Both probably thought they were saving the world. But which world, the third (Viet Nam) or the first (the U.S.)? And from what? For what reasons? They told me it had something to do with things like freedom and democracy. But everyone claimed to be fighting for those.

CARLOS

For in this hope we were saved. Now hope that is seen is not hope. For who hopes for what he sees?"
- Romans 8:24

We were sitting in a cafe sipping warm Victoria beer and eating cold rice and beans when Carlos put his finger to his ear.

"Escuche (Listen)," he said. "Bombas (Bombs)."

He looked toward the North. I listened intently. I had heard the same faint irregular thunder coming from the mountains the night before. But I had thought it was thunder. I was a little scared. Now it seemed close. I was glad I was returning to Managua in the morning. Carlos was also leaving in the morning - for his battalion in the mountains. He was on his monthly two day leave. Three days before a contra mortar had blown some shrapnel into his right forearm. He had wrapped a piece of shirt around it, but it didn't seem to do any good. The wound was blue and brown and still seeping. It hurt to look at it.

He looked young in his baggy Sandinista greens and worn hi-top tennis shoes. Or maybe he just didn't look like a soldier - like he could do what soldiers were supposed to do. But he didn't look or talk like a teenager either. He wanted to know why we were trying to overthrow his country - why he had to "defend his right to rice and beans and hope" - why his father and brother had died doing that - why he had to hug an AK-47 in the rain in the mountains instead of his girlfriend in the moonlight in Leon.

It was getting harder for me to understand Carlos' fluid Spanish. He looked tired too - probably from the beer. It started to rain. It did every day about this time. First, the rhythmic pinging on the corrugated metal roof - gradually growing into a relentless machinegunning - so loud I had to yell when asking Carlos what they did for protection during this season in the mountains.

"Nothing," he yelled back, "We have a lean-to and tents, but you still get wet...and sick."

The rain kept pounding. A mother yelled at her daughter to get inside ("Veni!") A dead gray dog that was lying on the side of the dirt main street was slowly turned on its other side by the growing current running along the curb. A man pushing a wooden cart full of mangos, firewood, and plaintain waved and smiled big - his strong, brown torso gleaming.

Carlos was still talking about freedom, but the rain and beer had brought my concentration to such a low that I couldn't keep out the details of village life, or stop my daydreams. I was wondering what Carlos, a good-looking seventeen year old, would be doing right now if he lived in the States. Playing tennis and golf and video games and going to the homecoming dance? Learning how to drive or play the piano? Going to a movie and wolfing down a pizza? Watching TV or working computers? He'd have more than rice and beans and hope anyway. But I wasn't sure if it would be that much better. He talked about freedom with a passion that I couldn't quite understand. He said if the contras were "freedom fighters," what was <u>he</u> fighting for?

"I don't know what communism is," he said finally, "but if it would help my mother and sisters get some food and clothes and a little piece of land, it might be a pretty good thing."

It was around 9:30, and the rain was back to a steady pinging. This made it easier to talk. But Carlos said he had to go. Absent-mindedly, I asked him if he didn't want to wait for the rain to stop. "Until June?" he said. We both laughed. I offered him my old black pop-up umbrella. He took it. I said I'd return in December. He'd leave word for me with his uncle. We'd try to get together. He grabbed his AK-47, opened my umbrella, and walked into the dripping darkness. I remained in the cafe for several hours – sipping beer, listening to the thunder, and wishing I could give Carlos protection from something besides the rain.

NAVIDAD
(CHRISTMAS)

As each has received a gift, employ it for one another, as good stewards of God's varied grace..."
- I Peter 4:10

Other than a few dim lights off in the fields, and an occasional unsettled rooster, it was dark and still when Manuel and I finally found the Hilario San Chez Farming Cooperative. It was Christmas Eve, and Manuel wanted to get back to his family in Managua before midnight. Since we were about 30 kilometers north of El Viejo, he had about a three hour drive remaining. So he dropped me in front of the old school (a barn), and pointed me in the direction of the house where he thought I was supposed to stay. I thanked him, pulled out my backpack, and watched the lights of his landrover bounce away over the rutted dirt road.

I sat down on a stump in front of the school. It didn't seem like Christmas Eve. It was only a quarter to ten - why was it so quiet? Where were the children? I was prepared for no snow or strings of colored lights or living rooms full of carefully wrapped presents and Better Homes and Gardens hors d'oeuvres; but didn't they celebrate at all? They must do something. They must have something they can give each other.

I discovered that they did, but it took me a long time to recognize these "gifts." They weren't wrapped carefully or colorfully enough. I didn't see the gift in the children's black hungry eyes, or in their parents' determined, hopeful sweat. I had wanted a direct equivalent to affluent North American "same as cash," "never needs batteries," "beats as it sweeps"

7

gifts. But there were none - no Sears, or L. L. Bean's, or Marshall Field's or specialized knick knack boutiques - no gift certificates or charge accounts. There was nothing but cotton fields, volcanoes, and lean, lost dogs straying in the dust. How could they have Christmas here?

The funny thing was that I'd gone to Nicaragua not only to learn, but because I had the idea that I had something to give - to the Nicaraguan people, to North Americans when I returned, to somebody. But at that point I couldn't give a thing. I was too concerned with Christmas at home; with my family and turkey and presents. I started to get a little depressed.

I had only been on the cooperative for about half an hour and I was already beginning to wonder about my rationale for coming. All my friends had told me that there were plenty of politics and poor people in the U.S. too. Why did I need to go to Nicaragua? What was I trying to prove? Why didn't I save the money for the air fare and donate it to the poor? Right then, sitting there with the moon, eating my banana, those seemed like pretty good questions.

I finally decided to wade into the darkness and try to find my house when I saw a light approaching from the field behind me.

"Hola."

"Hola," I said, and walked toward the low voice and still indistinguishable figure. A few more steps and I could see. It was a young man - probably late 20's. He had a coughing baby in his right arm and a bottle light (a kerosene soaked rag stuffed in a pop bottle) in his left hand. He was smiling and seemed excited. He explained that he was Eriberto and that I would be staying with him and his family for my week and a half on the cooperative.

We weaved down a path, through shoulder high weeds, the baby coughing and choking all the way. I couldn't figure out what was wrong. A couple of times it choked for several seconds and Eriberto stopped walking to pat its back. But he never said a word. After about ten minutes we arrived at his home – a small rusted metal and wooden shack. His wife, Santo, was waiting for me with Christmas dinner, a plate (palm leaf) full of hot rice and beans and fried plaintain. I ate quickly and collapsed in the hammock they had hung for me. Eriberto and Santo said "Feliz Navidad" (Merry Christmas) and disappeared with their son behind the divider that separated the room. I peeked through the crack along the wall to see that Eriberto, Santo and their five children were all going to sleep in a space smaller than mine, about six by twelve feet.

I woke in a cloud of smoke. Santo was cooking, and I was hanging right in the middle of the kitchen, only a few feet from the fire! Noticing my movement, she smiled, and then brought some hard sweet biscuits that she had made especially for Christmas, and a red plastic glass full of "cafe con leche" (hot milk with a little instant coffee and too much sugar stirred in).

I didn't have any idea what time it was, so I just lay there eating my Christmas biscuits and watched the morning come through the "front door" a rectangular opening in the metal. The sun was torching red on the horizon, beyond the sorghum fields and banana trees. Someone in a hut in the valley below us was making fire. The roosters were crowing like crazy. (No wonder everyone got up at daybreak). And a steady wind was picking up, which made the whole shack whine, and drew the smoke outside.

I was thinking about what I'd be doing just then if I were back in the States. Wake to the news on my digital alarm, get up and start my Mr. Coffee and the shower, shave with my Norelco, get the paper out of the door, decide on a flavor of cereal and jam, etc., etc. My technological world seemed so much more predictable and efficient. Here you had to depend on people, because there just wasn't anything else. No clocks, or radios, or TVs, or refrigerators, or cars, or garages, or garage door openers, or washing machines, not even electricity or running water.

It kind of reminded me of camping. I had been on backpack trips before where we'd done without running water and electricity for several days, but somehow this was different. We weren't trying to "get back to nature" or "to get away from it all." Because there was no "all" to leave or return to.

GOING FOR WATER

"Gargantuan industry and government, woven into an intricate computerized mechanism, leaves the person outside. The sense of participation is lost, the feeling that ordinary individuals influence important decisions vanishes, and people become separated and diminished."
— Martin Luther King, Jr.

We had a wooden shallow box, about four by four feet, to mix the cement in. It was simple. Ilatio and I would dump in two or three wheelbarrows full of sand, a couple of packages of cement, seven or eight pails of water and then mix it with shovels. It took the two of us about 25 minutes of hard scooping and mixing before one boxful was uniform enough to pour (by the bucket) into the new foundations. Each house took about five boxfuls. They were planning on 60-70 houses eventually. It struck me how much raw energy and time would be saved if they only had a cement mixer. It could mix a couple of boxfuls in a matter of minutes while Ilatio and I worked on something else. If they only had a little more technology, a little more of the "all."

But the mixing process seemed sophisticated compared to that of obtaining water (for the cement). For the last two days I had watched Eriberto and others roll down one after another of the rusted 100 gallon drums full of water, but never stopped to think where they had filled them. There weren't any spigots and they couldn't have gotten that much water at the well by bucket and pulley. On my third day there we finally ran out.

I knew we needed water to finish the rest of the foundations, but I was a little surprised when everyone stopped digging and climbed on the wagon. (There were three others working besides Ilatio and me that

13

day). They all seemed to know where we were going. I didn't, but I jumped on the wagon anyway, since I was anxious to find a reason to stop digging in the rock-hard clay with my ridiculously dull shovel.

"Adonde vamos? (Where are we going?)," I asked Julia, who had been laying block.

"Por agua, (For water.)" she replied.

Well I knew that, since we had the 12 drums with us. So I asked again. "Al rio," she said this time. We were going to the river.

Eriberto started up the Soviet made tractor (one of six the Sandinista government had given the cooperative) and we were off. The dirt road leading out of the cooperative was badly rutted, causing the empty water drums to bounce and rumble loudly. With this and the tractor engine and the wind it was impossible to talk. So everyone had retreated into their own world of relief - finally it was cool and we could sit down.

We turned right on the main gravel road, toward El Viejo and Chinandega, rolling and bumping past endless fields of sugar cane and cotton.

When we reached the river Eriberto veered off the main road, backing the back of the wagon right up to the river's edge. I still didn't get it. How were we going to get the river into the barrels? The openings were only about two inches in diameter. At first I thought that they'd drown them - that is force the barrel under the water, let it fill, then roll it out off the bottom. The problem with this was that they'd probably be too heavy to roll out, and it'd be nearly impossible to lift them onto the wagon.

Julia jumped off the back of the wagon into the hip deep water. Ilatio threw down four metal pails and splashed in after her. Julia handed me two pails full of water. Teetering and spilling, I turned to find Eriberto waiting for me with a metal funnel in one of the barrels. I emptied my pails. Huberto had just received his two pails from Ilatio. Due to the close quarters I accidentally bumped into him, causing him to spill. It was a little awkward at first, but after a few more trips, after we came to anticipate each other's movements a little better, our assembly line picked up speed. Slowly, the sound of the pouring water became less and less hollow and deep, until the barrel finally overflowed. Eriberto moved the funnel. It had taken us over 50 pailfuls and nearly 15 minutes to fill the first one - only 11 more to go.

After a little more than two hours all the barrels were full. But three were missing their screw-on lids. We stuffed wadded branches in these to keep the water loss at a minimum on the bumpy ride home.

It was so hot that we all decided to get wet. Eriberto and Ilatio could dogpaddle, but none of the rest knew how to swim. They waded out to their waists. I showed Eriberto how to do the crawl. He caught on quickly, except that it was hard for him to get used to turning his head to the side for air.

Later I noticed he was feeling along the bank for something - under the water. I swam up behind him to see what he was doing.

"Mira (Look)," he said.

He pulled out a bluish prehistoric looking thing with large pinchers and stuck it in front of my face. With its legs it was about the size of my clenched fist.

"What is it?" I asked, a little startled.

"Concha...para cena, (Crab...for dinner.)" he smiled, amused at my obvious anxiety.

He showed me how to hold it without getting pinched.

It was my turn. He took my hand and placed it over a softball-sized hole just under the water along the bank. He then took my other hand and placed it over another hole about two feet directly to the left.

"Cuidado (Careful)," he warned smiling.

I soon figured out that one hole was the crab's entrance and the other his exit. The problem was knowing which was which. Either you would hit the crab from behind, surprising him into scurrying out the other end into your waiting hand or net, or you would stick your hand in his face, into his pinchers.

I decided to try the one on the right. Expecting the worst, I slowly pushed my hand further into the hole. Everyone was watching now.

When I was nearly up to my elbow I felt something move.

"Yaaaaah!"

Wrong hole. Terrified, I yanked out my arm with the crab locked firmly on my thumb. I waved my hand wildly trying to shake it off. But I couldn't. Finally Eriberto grabbed my hand and the crab. He bit the leg in two just below the pincher. It slipped off my thumb and fell into the water. Julia, Ilatio, and Huberto were shaking with laughter on the opposite bank.

Eriberto put the crab in a bucket with the five or six others he had caught. It would be enough for dinner, with rice and beans.

Ilatio threw me a hunk of soap. I then noticed that everybody had started bathing. Not wanting to miss the opportunity, I soaped every inch of my body, and my clothes as well. I put them on wet to keep cool, but they dried quickly in the wind. Everyone was moving toward the wagon, so I figured it was time to go. We wheeled the heavy drums of water toward the center, and sat around the perimeter, our feet dangling over the edge.

On the way home, the slow dusty rumble toward the falling sun, I was thinking about the day, about how much simpler the campesinos lives would be if they only had a spigot on the cooperative - a little more of the "all." One person could run a hose from the spigot directly into the mixing box with a minimum of time and energy. Instead, the five of us had "wasted" the entire afternoon at the river, and we'd have to go again in a week or so.

But I had learned how to catch crabs, and Eriberto how to do the crawl. I had also gotten to know Huberto and Julia better - despite our mutual shyness and my stumbling Spanish. Huberto had explained why the cotton crop had failed, and Julia why all of her six younger brothers and sisters had been born premature. I had taught them both how to "triple skip" rocks on the river, and the first verse of "This Land is Your Land" in Spanish.

ON TIME

"To reduce life to the matter of getting things done, all in this name of practicality by which every thought and deed is either justified or condemned, makes one-dimensional persons of us all. By focusing on purpose it forecloses the possibility of everything that is not functionally productive, such as prayer.

— Dorothee Soëlle

On the day before I left the cooperative I gave Eriberto and his family a gift — a little, round, red digital stick-on clock, that I had gotten at Osco's Drugs for $1.99. They were elated and immediately stuck it on the rusty corrugated dividing wall, on the kitchen side. Santo kept telling me how much she had wanted a clock, and how expensive they were.

While I was packing later that afternoon I remember thinking how funny and out of place it looked. A bright red plastic sign of technology stuck amid the primitive greys and browns, amid the rust and dirt and wood. The only other thing they had that was nearly as technologically advanced was the red plastic glass, which they of course insisted that only I use while I was there.

I had given them a little bit more of the "all." Or had I? I had only seen one clock on the entire cooperative, and it was broken. I hadn't seen any wristwatches. So even though Eriberto now had a modern digital measure of time, the rest of the cooperative still moved to the rhythm of the sun and roosters. It wouldn't make any difference if Eriberto knew it was 5:56 a.m. or 6:00 a.m. or 6:08 a.m., because the rest of the campesinos were going to meet at the tractor on the hill to begin work when the sun came up.

I couldn't help but wonder about almuerzo (lunch) too. How did they all know when to stop without a noon whistle or watch? Midday seemed even less exact than daybreak.

I found out my first day in the fields. Ilatio and I were picking cotton. It was hot and windy and we were both thirsty and wondering what time it was, if it was close to lunch. Finally we heard the bell on the hill, Eriberto hitting a piece of dangling iron with a hammer. Lunch time! As we walked we waved in three others who hadn't heard the bell. They had been working in a field on the other side of the road. We all walked up the hill to the school, washed at the well, and sat in the shade. It was Maria and Roberto's turn to cook that day. They had come in early and prepared rice, tomatoes and tortillas for everyone.

I remember thinking what it would be like if we had all had Seiko digital alarm wristwatches. No one would have had to tell us when to stop working. We wouldn't even have had to look at our watches; the alarm would sound at exactly 12:00. Then we would all go wherever we wanted, have our lunch, and come back when the 1:00 alarm sounded. We wouldn't need to rely on Eriberto or on anything else as inexact and unmeasurable as the sun and human intuition.

On one of my last days on the cooperative I woke to find Eneyda, Santo's pregnant sister, slumping against one of the shack's support poles. I had only seen her once before, at her house by the banana grove, but I knew something was wrong. She was pale, sweating and said she felt weak. She had a fever, but since we didn't have a thermometer my first world mind couldn't quite believe it. I couldn't rely only on her symptoms or my intuition. I needed to know that her body temperature exceeded 98.6 degrees. I needed numerical confirmation.

Santo got Eneyda a cool wet rag for her forehead. I gave her a couple of aspirin and told her to keep the rest of the bottle. For the next three days she returned to our house daily, bringing a different gift (plantain, yuca, or homemade rolls) for me each time in appreciation for my wonder drug. I had given her a little more of the "all," and she had given me complete trust - in my nonexistent medical expertise.

And somehow I guess I had thought that my little red clock could do the same thing for Eriberto. That it could rescue him from his primitive solar dependency and put him in control. I had thought that if I could only give "digital punctuality" (and a spigot) to Eriberto and the rest of the campesinos that they would begin to move toward a more technological, and thus, a less painful life. It was at least the first step.

Eriberto had agreed to take me to Chinandega on the tractor the next morning (an hour long trip), where I was to meet an express bus to Ocotol at 7:00 a.m. That night I went to bed hoping that one of us would wake up by 5:30, so we'd have plenty of time. But I didn't have a wristwatch (I'd left it in Managua), let alone an alarm clock.

When I woke it was pitch black and someone was moving near me. It was Eriberto. He was trying to read the digital clock. He couldn't find the bottlelight and finally removed the clock from the divider and walked outside. I assumed he was going to try moonlight. He returned in moments, his voice sounding confused.

"Dice son las 12:30...pero, el cielo esta demasiado claro. Debemos salir ahora. (It says 12:30, but the sky is too light. We should leave now.)."

I went to the doorway. The moon was full, but the sky didn't look any lighter. Still, I wasn't going to argue. Even if it was 12:30 a.m., I could hang

21

out in Chinandega for a couple of hours. I didn't want to insult Eriberto.

He was still standing there glaring at the clock.

"It stopped beating," he said finally.

I didn't know the Spanish word for "beat," so I went over to see what he meant.

He was right. It was broken. The pulsing colon between the 12 and the 30 had stopped. Digital time was standing still.

So we still didn't know what time it was. At least I didn't. And I think that I may have even been secretly hoping that it really was 1:00 a.m. or 2:00 a.m., so my clock would be closer to the real time than Eriberto's intuitive, natural clocks.

I went back inside to get my backpack. When I emerged Eriberto was already sitting on the sputtering tractor. He seemed concerned that we were late. I had my doubts though. It still looked like midnight.

I climbed into the cab, Eriberto shifted into gear, and we lunged forward up the hill, toward the road.

"Mira, (Look)," Eriberto said when we finally reached the top of the hill. For the first time we could see the eastern sky, which had just begun to lighten. A faint orange haze was starting to seep over the horizon. It was around 6:00. Eriberto was right. We were on time.

ON TIME IN MANAGUA

Here comes another one. Nope. The wooden sign in the window says 114. I was in a hurry. I wouldn't have waited so long for the route 118 bus if the woman next to me hadn't promised me that it would come. And if she and about 12 others hadn't sat there with me in the same dust and sun and diesel exhaust for the same 46 minutes. Their patience and durability were encouraging, but by 1:30 I was beginning to have my doubts. I was beginning to think "taxi."

Here comes another one. This time everyone stands up, seeming to sense this is it. It is. There's an 18 painted in red on the lower left corner of the windshield. It's a rusted Bluebird schoolbus, and just like all the others it's jammed full with over 100 passengers. There are more bodies squeezed in the aisle than sitting. Fifteen or twenty arms are sticking out the windows because there's no room for them inside. Seven or eight kids are "white-knuckling" it on the outside, clinging to the remaining chrome molding and ladder on back like magnets on a refrigerator.

I wedge my way in the door, stick a wadded 10 cordoba bill in the driver's hand, but am pushed deeper into the heap before I get change. I fight to make a space for myself. I can't. I notice a thin toothless man sitting near a window. He's giving a young child a drink from a knotted plastic baggie full of ice water. One woman next to me has a couple of live hens in a bag, and keeps mashing them into my back whenever the bus starts or stops. She looks at me apologetically.

This is public transportation in Managua. For only three cordobas and a little patience and humor you can go clear across the city. Through the acres and

acres and rows and rows of patched corrugated steel and wooden homes, of darting lizards and squealing pigs and children, of boney listless dogs and ferocious insects, of radios and roosters and rumbling wooden carts, of smoky delicious street vendors and mountains of pineapples and plantain, of endless games of pickup baseball, and of too many teenagers dressed in green trying to look like soldiers.

And after a week or so of riding the buses it all starts to look the same - like it doesn't really matter where you get on or off. There's always a basket of mangos, a ballgame, and an AK-47 waiting for you. Everything melts into a huge watercolor swish of poverty and revolution - and sometimes hope.

But today I can't see anything. I am straining to look out a window to see if we're close to the Plaza Espana, where I was supposed to meet a friend at 1:00 for lunch. The bus pulls to a stop.

"Aqui! Aqui! (Here! Here!)" shouts the chicken woman, whom I had asked to tell me when we arrived at the plaza. I fight toward the door, but even in my frenzy can only squirm three or four feet closer. Other people see my desperate expression and try to make space for the gringo. They can't. The bus is off again with a hot carbonic hiss and I'm still in the middle of the pack.

As we sway and sweat between lanes, attempting to avoid some oxen and a stalled car, I continue to writhe closer, hoping I can reach the suction of the exit vacuum near the door and be spewed out at the next stop. We slow down.

"Con permiso! Con permiso! (Pardon me. Pardon me.)" I say for the 20th time. (This is a common and accepted expression on the buses which really means, "Excuse me for knocking you out of the way.")

The bus stops. I'm close to the door and practically on the chicken lady's shoulders. She bangs her way forward. I surge to the right of her block at the last instant, breaking into the daylight. Bewildered but free, I am finally back in the panorama, or at least a hot dusty piece of it.

Lost and late I begin walking. After ten minutes or so I see the Plaza Espana, and finally arrive at the park where I was supposed to have met Orlando 1 1/2 hours earlier.

I am amazed to see him still sitting on a park bench casually reading El Nuevo Diario (newspaper).

When he sees me he looks up and smiles.

"It's good to see you," he says grabbing my hand. "Did you get anything for lunch yet?"

SAFE AT HOME

"Do not be conformed to this world, but be transformed by the renewal of your mind..."
- Romans 12:2

The Intercontinental Hotel looks like a pyramid with the top lopped off. It's the closest you can get to North America in Nicaragua.

Today there is an elderly campesino out front cutting and selling coconuts. He can clean the hull off one in less than a minute with his machete. But those who stay at the "Inter" want the hulls left on. They want them for souvenirs, to set on their mantles or coffee tables, not because they are hungry or thirsty. So he sells mostly uncuts.

The smiling servant opens the door and the cool whoosh sucks me from the surrounding dusty myriad of poverty into an air-conditioned oasis of polished wood and piled carpet, of lush potted greenery and sparkling chandeliers.

There are important looking people here. Khakied journalists smoking U.S. brand cigarettes and looking determined. Businessmen in their newest pastel tennis outfits reading their personal copies of the Wall Street Journal and looking wealthy. They are all moving toward the dining room for the luncheon buffet or a frosty beer in the lounge.

I hear a woman from the Boston Globe complaining about the room service. "You'd think for $45.00 a night I could get a little ice when I needed it."

Her friend looks European. He is dark and has an immaculately trimmed beard.

"So what do you expect, Margaret? We're in the third world," he counters.

But somehow I didn't find the Inter to be all that characteristic of the third world. The buffet luncheon was a whole room full of food - more than I've ever seen: skewered steak, broiled shrimp and snapper and five other entrees, freshly cut melons, papayas, oranges, pineapples, and mangos, about 15 or 20 side dishes, and finally the dessert tray: delicately layered chocolate cakes, flans, pastries, and tortes. But it was more than just the quantity of food. The waiters and food preparers seemed obsessed with how the buffet looked - that it was visually pleasing to the customers. They sprayed the fruit to keep it looking shiny and succulent. They replaced trays of food before they were empty because they looked too messy or mangled. Everything was correctly arranged and color coordinated.

Upon leaving I noticed another sector of the Inter's clientele that I had ignored before - probably because I belong to it. These are the tourists, the world vagabonds, who have come from the U.S. and Canada and Europe to see a revolution first hand. They are easy to spot with their baggy cotton clothes, straw hats, and broken Spanish. They tote bright colorful woven bags full of revolutionary books and pamphlets. They can afford the supply of new books and the buffet because the dollar and most other forms of Western European money are worth a great deal in Nicaragua.

The buffet cost 4,800 cordobas. A big new paper bound book such as the Bible or the Abbreviated Works of Karl Marx (two of the most common and abundant books in Managua's state run grocery stores) would run about 2,200. One U.S. dollar is worth 1,900. You can buy a pineapple or a dozen oranges in the market for 650. A bottle of soda is around 400 and a beer around 600 if you can find any. So things were cheap if you were a Yankee. It wouldn't be hard to get used to spending a lot of time at the Inter.

But at that particular time, having just returned from a month on the cooperative with Eriberto and Santo, the Inter and the buffet had been quite a shock. Not because I was sacrificial, or like eating only rice and beans, but because of the contrast between the few haves, with their cool, quenching luxury, and the massive number of have-nots, who scrounged in the dusty heat around the Inter like roosters. On the cooperative everybody had been scrounging. And even though I had changed money in Managua at 1,900 to 1, and had taken plenty of it with me, there was nothing to spend it on. There was no buffet to buy.

The next morning I was to meet a friend at the airport. Since I was staying in a hostel near the Inter, and it was the only place to get a paper and find out where to get a taxi for the airport, I stopped back in. I couldn't help but notice the breakfast buffet as I walked by the entrance to the dining room. It was no less lavish than the luncheon; a shiny metallic turntable of steaming eggs and French toast and pastries and fruits, all for 3,000 cordobas. Nearly the same clientele was there. Someone new was complaining, because there was no ice, because the milk and fruit were cool rather than cold.

While I was washing up in the bathroom I was again thinking about life on the cooperative, about the little wooden box with a hole in it in the field behind our shack. In comparison this place was Buckingham Palace. This was the first time I had seen toilet paper and soap (and free!) in a public place. And this had to be the only hot air hand dryer in the whole country.

At the corner where I was waiting for a taxi there was another coconut vender, selling cut coconuts (or uncuts to an occasional tourist) for 400 Cordobas. Since I didn't need any more souvenirs I bought a cut one to eat. I wasn't hungry, but it was entertainment while waiting. After five or ten minutes I figured out which part I was supposed to eat, though I still had problems separating the meat from the hull. Finally I gave up. Minutes later a couple of kids came and sat down beside me. We started talking and I noticed them eyeing the coconut. I offered it to them. They thanked me, broke it open and began eating and laughing.

* * *

It is Sunday morning but no imposing organ tones rise from Managua's oldest and largest cathedral, no confessions nor "Hail Mary's" nor fidgeting, sweating children aching to escape the heat and quiet. The gold-inlayed, ceramic saints, oak pews, bright, intricately stained windows, and red velvet altar are all gone now, victims of the 1972 earthquake.

The high arched ceiling is now a crisscross of bent iron ribs that throw a changing geometry of shadows on the sanctuary three stories below. I climb to the top floor, the second balcony, to get a better view of the cathedral's new function - an indoor (no wind) baseball stadium for the neighborhood kids. Since it's Sunday there'll be a double, or maybe even a triple header today. They're warming up now - shagging flies or trying to handle grounders off the bumpy dirt floor. More and more kids arrive until there are 16, enough for two teams of eight. They walk off the distances and set down the cardboard bases. After some shoving and laughing they pick teams.

The first pitch looks low but the batter takes a half swing - a high fly. It drifts close to the rusted skeleton roof. Manuel, who is standing on the remains of a stone altar table in center field, makes the play. One down. Next batter. He's big. Everyone takes a few steps back. Two balls. He swings this time. A hard line drive ricochets off a tile inlay of John the Baptist on the second balcony. Some crumbled tile and dust drift to the ground. Foul ball. Another pitch and another foul line drive - about 20 feet to the left. This time St. Francis takes one in the gut. More dust and tile fall.

The game continues, but then I notice a curl of smoke and glint of a flame way back in the shadows of the first balcony, on the other side of the building. Probably some kids fooling around. But I decide to check it out. Maybe I can get some good pictures.

I climb down the stairs to the second floor, go out to the edge of the balcony and look around. Yeah, it's a fire all right, and some people are scattered around it. But it's too dark to tell what they're doing. I walk around the balcony. The sun is almost overhead now and is pouring light on the baseball game. Someone just wiped out on the turn at first and is tagged out - there's a big argument.

I can smell the fire and make my way to where I think it should be. But the entry to this particular area is blocked by a huge corroded piece of corrugated metal. I notice a hole in the makeshift wall.

About fifteen away, amid the revolving smoky shadows, I can make out a young mother sitting on a broken hunk of concrete nursing her child. Her husband has another child in his arm and is squatting over the fire, stirring a can of something that is close to boiling over. It looks like yuca. A bench and a large frayed hammock are near the opposite wall. A small wooden cross made from two sticks and a piece of string has been tied to a pipe and hangs over the hammock.

After staring awhile I realize that I have stumbled on to somebody's living room and move on, not wanting to disturb their breakfast.

As I walked back around the balcony and down the stairs I was thinking how odd it seemed that someone was "camping" in a cathedral - that they made a fire and ate there. Or that they played baseball there. I had thought that only holy things were supposed to happen in a cathedral.

When I turned out of the stairway on to the ground floor I noticed a distinguished looking man leaning on the wall watching the baseball game. He caught my eye because he wasn't Nicaraguan. He looked American.

"Hola," I said.

"I'm sorry. I don't speak Spanish," he replied.

"Me neither," I confided. "Where are you from?"

"Chicago. I'm just down here for a week...kind of a fact finding mission."

I wanted to know more, like what kind of facts you could find in English.

"I'm a priest," he went on, "I'm down here with five other priests and a few Protestant pastors. We're trying to find out if the Sandinistas are really allowing for religious freedom."

He continued, "Before we came we did a lot of reading. I read all about how Christian Base Communities were crucial in the insurrection against Somoza. But not one of the books ever explained how these so called Christians could take up arms and kill and steal in the name of God. The problem now is that none of the real Christians have any power. All of their possessions were expropriated. A lot went to Florida. All you have now are a lot of communists - trained by the USSR and Cuba. I think it's a shame that the Sandinistas can keep shoving all this socialist/communist doctrine down the throats of the true believers that remain here."

He wasn't worried about holding anything back.

"But what about Liberation Theology?" I countered. "You know...the stuff about Sandino being like Christ...a poor revolutionary who was assassinated because he tried to liberate his people?"

"That's bunk. Sandino had nothing to do with Christ. He was more like Robin Hood. Christ was not a revolutionary, he was the son of God. Politics and religion just don't mix. I think that's the one thing we've learned in the States that the rest of the world could benefit from. Every time you start trying to mix the spiritual and divine with political reality, you have problems - the revolutions and riots - sometimes even civil war. Are you going to tell me that's what God wants? That people should kill and steal and break God's laws so they can establish their own? Look at this cathedral. It was beautiful once - with stained glass and fine wood and gold. Why wasn't it ever rebuilt? It was the home of God. Now it's a dirty baseball diamond."

He went on for another half hour. After he left, I stayed and watched the last game. It was a round robin; the two losing teams were playing now. Some of the things the priest had said bothered me. I knew they hadn't rebuilt the cathedral because it was still on the fault line of the earthquake that had destroyed it. But as I watched the kids playing ball and noticed more smoke rising from the second balcony I had to wonder if it might have been a good thing. If the cathedral wasn't serving God and the people of the neighborhood now. If healthy physical entertainment and shelter for a family weren't just as holy as polished gold and wood and stained glass. If there might be some of Christ's body in a piece of yuca, and his blood in a knee skinned in a slide toward home.

35

COMMUNION

"As they were eating, he took bread, and blessed, and broke it, and gave it to them, and said, 'Take; this is my body.' And he took a cup, and when he had given thanks he gave it to them, and they all drank of it. And he said to them, 'This is my blood of the covenant, which is poured out for many.'"
 — Mark 14:22-24

When Dolores, my assumed Nicaraguan mother, had said her Padre was "un sacerdote revolucionario" (a revolutionary priest), I was confused. It seemed like a conflict in terms. Would he be armed with the communist manifesto and an AK-47, or the Bible and a rosary?

In a later interview he convinced me that he could make use of all four. He explained the split in the Nicaraguan Roman Catholic Church. How he had evolved from the traditional Rome-backed wing of the church, which now denounced him. How he had come to believe in a "theology of liberation," which holds up the massive peasant majority and their socio-political transformation as a crucial part of the Christian tradition and focus of religious practice.

"Christ the Savior did not only die for our sins. He was tortured and crucified because he preached liberation for the poor," he explained. "You can see the parallel with our struggle for liberation. Rome has been replaced by the U.S."

I had recently read where several priests from the traditional wing of the church had refused to perform burials for Sandinista soldiers killed in battle, many of whom had been life long members of these churches. These priests claimed that even though the teen-aged soldiers had been baptized and confirmed in the Catholic church, they were now Sandinistas, and thus atheists doomed to hell.

* * *

A teenager in tattered Sandinista greens comes whirling in stumbling circles through the open doors of Dolores' church. Arms out straight and giggling, he spins and teeters down the main aisle like a drunken top, finally expiring at the rough hewn wooden altar in the middle of the church. He falls to his knees laughing.

The Padre who is blessing the bread and wine, seems a little confused. A man in the first pew goes up and tries to pull the boy out. The boy stops laughing and looks scared. He puts both his hands over his head. The Padre stops the man. He sits down with the boy in front of the altar, puts his arm around him, and whispers something in his ear. The Mass continues with the boy squatting near the altar, watching.

* * *

At home after the Mass, while starting the fire for supper, Dolores explains that she has always had to deal with the division in the church. She grew up in Granada, a wealthy conservative city 35 miles north of Managua. She had never understood why the wealthy had so much, while she had to scrimp and barter just to get eggs or milk a couple of times a week. Her mother said if they only had faith God would deliver them.

But everyday Dolores walked through the "faithful" section on her way to the market for rice and beans - past the bright green manicured lawns, the polished tile walks, and the shiny new European cars. She could hear them laughing knowingly behind their iron gates with their tinkling rum and Cokes. She could smell their cigarettes and sizzling meat. She imagined their ice cream and blue jeans and refrigerators and stoves. And then she was home, at her plywood shack, her four little brothers and baby sister sitting patiently in the dirt, waiting for some stimulation. Her mother was still on the same wooden stool, holding a Bible and telling her to have faith. But she couldn't. She couldn't kiss the ceramic saints anymore. She couldn't walk on her knees down the cathedral aisle. She couldn't put any more cordobas in the wooden box in front of the Virgin Mary, or at least not until her brothers had some shoes.

* * *

From my position in the fourth row I can see the boy's face. He is mumbling to himself and looks confused. I hear someone behind me say that his name is Rigoberto, a boy from the neighborhood that has returned recently from the border, from his required two year stint with the Sandinistas. He was wounded (brain damage due to lodged shrapnel, I later discovered) and has had problems readjusting.

* * *

"I agree with my Mom...God does have a plan," Dolores explained while rapidly pat-patting corn meal into tortillas. "But I don't think it's that me and my family or anybody else should go hungry. After a while you get tired of waiting - of looking through the gates. You know it never really bothered me so much that they had all those things, it was just the idea that they were better, that God likes them better. I never understood that."

* * *

Rigoberto stares hard at the Padre. He leans forward out of his squat into a kneel. But he makes this movement too quickly and bumps his head on the altar. He holds his head and begins to cry. The congregation is oblivious. They come forward and form a line for communion. The Padre gives bread to each. The boy looks confused as the people file by him, returning to their seats with their hands clasped in front of their chests.

* * *

Dolores' kitchen is outdoors in the back part of the house - a smoldering fire, a spigot, and a collection of dented pots and pans. The beans are bubbling now, and the tortillas greasy hot and crispy. She spoons a steaming brown heap of beans on a tortilla and puts it on a plate in front of me. There is no running water on Friday so I dip some from a nearby pail. The hot, dusty afternoon wind has given way to a cool breeze and light rain. Dolores serves herself and we continue talking amid the flickering shadows.

"I wish my mother could have heard the sermon tonight. Do you remember when he said 'in acting as Christians we become Christians'?"

I did, since that was the focus of his homily.

"That's why my Mom doesn't understand. She believes in divine providence. She thinks she's a good Christian because she always carries her rosary, says daily penance to all the saints stationed around the cathedral, and never doubts or questions her faith or the pope. The problem was after a lifetime of suffering her God didn't make any sense to me. I lost hope."

Dolores takes a big bite of beans and tortilla, looks surprised, then fans her mouth. She washes it down with some water and continues.

"My Mom can't even read. That makes it tough to get much out of the Bible. It's o.k. to have faith in the pope and the Catholic hierarchy. It's good that they give alms to the poor. But the Padre is saying that the poor deserve more than alms, a lot more. That we learn about our faith through our suffering and acting to change it. We need more than rituals and statues and wafers and wine. We need rice and beans and medication and clean water and books. My children and I can read now. That may be the most 'religious' experience of our lives."

* * *

The Padre gives bread to the last one in line. He then walks over to Rigoberto, who is still squatting a few feet from the altar. He kneels and offers the boy bread. As he takes it the Padre whispers "the body of Christ." The boy chews the bread, smiles and makes a distorted sign of the cross on his chest. He looks strangely satisfied as he wanders through the sanctuary looking for an empty seat. Some members of the congregation glare at him in disapproval.

* * *

The rain has picked up so Dolores and I go inside.

"Some don't like the Padre. They think he's too liberal. Some would say that he shouldn't have given Rigoberto communion tonight – that he shouldn't offer Christ's body to a Sandinista soldier, let alone a crazy one. They think Rigoberto isn't worthy anymore. Well, he is a soldier, and he is a little crazy, but you saw him take the bread. He knew what it meant."

While lying awake that night I thought about Rigoberto. I thought about the priests who had somehow determined that Sandinista soldiers could not be Christians. I thought about why they were fighting. Dolores had lost her son, Rudolfo, in a contra attack near the Honduran border a couple of years earlier. I had asked her if she felt her son's death was worthwhile, if their cause was worth dying for.

"Is our existence worthwhile?" she asked with confusion in her eyes.

"Mira (Look)," she said, pointing to a St. Francis medallion and small crucifix around her neck.

I asked her where she got it.

"It was Rudolfo's. He never took it off. I don't either."

Her voice was shaky.

"I need it now. It reminds me why I'm here," she had finally said wiping her eyes. "It gives me strength."

As I lay sweating in my hammock that night I couldn't help but wonder if Rigoberto didn't take communion for the same reasons.

TAKING PONELOYA

And when he had ceased speaking, he said to Simon, 'Put out into the deep and let your nets down for a catch.' And Simon answered, 'Master we toiled all night and took nothing. But at your word I will let down the nets.' And when they had done this they enclosed a great shoal of fish; and as their nets were breaking, they beckoned to their partners in the other boat to come and help them."
                                                  - Luke 5:4-7

I watch in disbelief as the wooden boat leaves the cove and heads out into the ocean, into the pink sunrise and six foot waves. Marco is in the bow and Emilio in the stern, manning the motor, an awkwardly sidemounted Johnson outboard. The rough hewn boat hits wave after wave head on. A large wave nearly stands the boat on end, then the hull crashes down in the next valley. I wonder how they hold on. This continues only for a few minutes though. After a few careful swerves and dodges, they are out of it, and on the open water.

Around 4:00 p.m. everyone in Poneloya seems to be moving toward the cove. The village is a half mile long row of wooden shacks and brick and plaster homes running parallel to the shoreline. Since this is the only street, the migration is even more obvious. I walk by a woman who is scrubbing clothes with rocks in the creek that runs by her shack. She has laid her child on a wooden bench in the shade and shoos flies that hover near or light on its face. She notices me and waves.

"Ya? Ya? El barco?" she says so quickly I can't understand. Confused, I smile and wave back good-naturedly. A few steps later I realize she was asking me if the boat has returned yet.

An old man sits on the stone steps on his home, reading the Barricada (the Sandinista newspaper) and whistling an unfamiliar tune.

"Yahnkee. Yahnkee," he says and laughs. He only has four or five teeth and is sucking on a cigar.

His joking unnerves me a little, even though I know he's kidding. It reminds me how out of place I am. That even though I picked coffee and cut sugar, lived with a peasant family both on the farming cooperative and in Managua, traveled by bus rather than taxi, and ate rice and beans and plantain rather than in restaurants, I'm still just a damned tourist. I'm going home to multi-leveled shopping centers and sixteen lane highways. That's the difference. Yankees can leave. And we visit when we want to. This guy wouldn't be coming to the U.S. out of curiosity.

"Veni," he says.

I go up and sit beside him.

"Mira," he says smiling and pointing to a headline, which I translate to read, "Aid Passes: Preparations for U.S. Invasion Begin."

Like always, the U.S. pervades the Nicaraguan press. I shrug my shoulders. I don't have any answers. He seems amused, offers me a cigar, and looks at me carefully.

"Porque viene aqui? (Why did you come here?)," he asks in a curious tone.

I try to explain that I just wanted to see the place, to see what we were defending, or fighting for, to - as all the language schools and left-wing church tour brochures say - "see the revolution first hand."

"Que bueno (That's good.)," he says, "Pero porque no nos mandan alguien de Washington? (But why don't you send us someone from Washington?)."

He laughs hard, and then, before I can respond, launches into an in-depth explanation of how he had gotten his cigars. How his brother, who works on a tobacco plantation near Esteli, sent him a handful every month.

"Son mejores que los Cubanos (They're even better than the Cuban ones)," he says.

"Como se llama?" I finally ask.

"Frederico," he smiles.

Two children run by us. They have been kicking a can back and forth between themselves since they left their home at the other end of the street. We have heard them coming for some time. The boy gives the can an extra hard boot and it goes off the street into a puddle along the side of the road. His older sister kicks it out of the water and gets splattered with mud in the process. They both laugh and run on ahead, after the can.

Like the other children at Poneloya, I'm struck by their size, particularly in contrast to the kids on the farming cooperative, where I had worked. These kids are nine or ten, according to Fredrico. But they are bigger than many of the teenagers on the cooperative. And they don't have any blatant signs of malnutrition, no blond streaks in their hair, nor protruding bellies.

I ask Frederico why.

"Hay bastante pescado para todo aqui, (There's plenty of fish for everyone here)," he says. "En el campo no hay bastante carne (But in the country there's not enough meat)."

47

That made sense. There just wasn't much protein on the cooperative.

Frederico says we can talk more later. I continue down the street. Two teenage boys are sharpening long butcher knives on a stone and testing them on a mango leaf. They put their knives in a plastic five gallon bucket, and start toward the cove. A little ways ahead of them a man and woman leave their home. The man is carrying a machete, the woman a couple of large metal pails in each hand. They clang together with each step.

There is a little breeze off the ocean as I near the cove. Otherwise it is hot and still. The rutted, asphalt street ends abruptly in the scorching sand. After a few steps I realize my bare feet can't take it, so I tear off for the shoreline. The fifteen or so people gathered there get a kick out of this. Still laughing, they make room for me in the shade of some palm trees.

Around 5:00 p.m. Emilio and Marco arrive. They cut the motor and coast into shore. Those with knives wade out to the boat. I follow. I am relieved when Emilio says "Hola," since I don't know any of the others very well.

The bottom of the boat is full of red snapper, scrod, small hammerhead and sand sharks, and other fish I don't recognize. Many are still flapping. It takes the six men an hour to filet the eighty or so fish. After explaining where and how to make the cuts, Emilio lets me try a hammerhead that was overlooked. The head comes off with two quick angled movements of the razor sharp knife. I gut it with one pass along the belly. We throw the severed tails, guts and shark heads (the shark heads are the only ones they remove, since they aren't considered edible) on the bank, which some pigs promptly devour.

It seems that every family has sent a representative to get supper. Now there are twenty-five or so gathered around the catch. Wide-eyed little kids and their bossy big brothers and sisters take a snapper or a scrod home in a pail or hooked through the gill on a branch. Eneyda, Emilio's eight year old sister, chooses a weak branch and it breaks, causing the fish to drop to the street. She comes back to the shore to wash it off, and this time carries the five pound snapper home cradled in her arms.

After rinsing the blood out of their shirts and cleaning their knives and buckets, Emilio and the other fisherman also head home. They too drift down the street with their supper on a stick, toward the same pink haze to which they woke.

I remain on the beach until all but an orange sliver of the sun has slipped below the horizon. Around 8:30 I head back to Emilio's for supper. As we sit outside and watch the large skewered snapper sizzle over the fire the stars begin to brighten. Emilio asks if they look different to me here than at home.

"Se parecen lo mismos," I say.

He smiles and seems glad they look the same.

We continue to watch the fish and the fire, lost in thought. I wonder what Emilio would do if the marines really did come some day, like the <u>Barricada</u> and Frederico had predicted. If they <u>took</u> Poneloya as a strategic beachhead and subdued these communist fishermen. In my naive idealism I can't help but dream, that maybe, like me, some of the marines would be <u>taken</u> - by the children's twilight games of "kick the can," the toothless cigar-smoking philosopher, the sleeping babies and their sweating mothers, Emilio and Marco's gravity-defying boat, the flopping shiny fish and swift agile knives, the tireless gleaming brown bodies, the soft eternal lapping of the tide, and the quiet hopeful rhythm of the day.

49

SELLING POP

"The women of my people you drive out from their pleasant houses; from their young children you take away my glory forever."

— Micah 2:9

Flora sells Pepsi and Coke in Leon. Every morning except Sunday she limps from her home, a dirt-floored hallway with a bed, to the town square. Though the trip is only about a mile it takes her nearly 45 minutes. This is because on the same walk, nearly seven years earlier (June 2, 1979), she was the victim of a helicopter bombing attack by Somoza's national guard.

Her leg had been much worse - little more than a useless appendage that dragged along behind. But since the surgery at the Leon Medical School in 1983 it is much better. She no longer needs crutches and can spend the entire day on her feet selling without much pain.

When the sun shines there are 25 or 30 other vendors on the square, all trying to earn enough to buy rice and beans and tortillas for themselves and their children. On good days they may be able to afford some meat or milk or bread.

Flora can usually make enough to buy a plastic half liter bag of milk five days a week. This is a priority since she has a two year old at home. Her other two girls are six and eleven, and can get along without it she says.

"For every pop I sell I make 80 cordobas. I buy them for 270 and sell them for 350," she continues.

Since bottles are a valuable commodity in Nicaragua, Pepsi, and other drinks, are sold in plastic "bolsas"

(bags). The vendor chips off a hunk of ice, sticks it in a baggie, pours in the bottle of pop, and knots it.

On a typical day, Flora's time is divided between bagging "gaseosas" (pop) for passersby, and selling at the bus stop, right across the street. The bus stop is a block long chaotic struggle between vendors trying to make a sale, and passengers fighting to get a seat. It is a good place to sell because there are a lot of hungry, thirsty people in a small area. But there is an even better place to sell with a more concentrated and captive audience: inside the buses that are about to leave.

Today there are three buses waiting, two south to Managua, and one north to Chinandega and Corinto. There are of course no seats left and the aisles are packed with people and fence posts and melons and baskets and bags full of mangos and lemons and plantain and chickens and pigs. Yet still the drivers wait, trying to pack another five or ten people on each bus.

Now the vendors wade in. They pry their way through the sticky impatient bodies, hoping to sell to the already weary travelers. They offer gaseosas, a bag of yuca and crispy fried pig back, fried plaintain chips, a refresco (a bag full of a cool fruit drink), or a gooey hunk of coconut candy as a diversion for the long ride to come.

Despite her handicap, Flora often sells inside the buses. But today they are just too full, so she circles them on the outside, selling to the arms that stick money at her through the windows. After fifteen minutes or so her eight bags of Pepsi and Coke are gone and she returns to her stand with an empty tray.

One driver is finally satisfied that his bus is full enough and leaves for Managua. The others follow

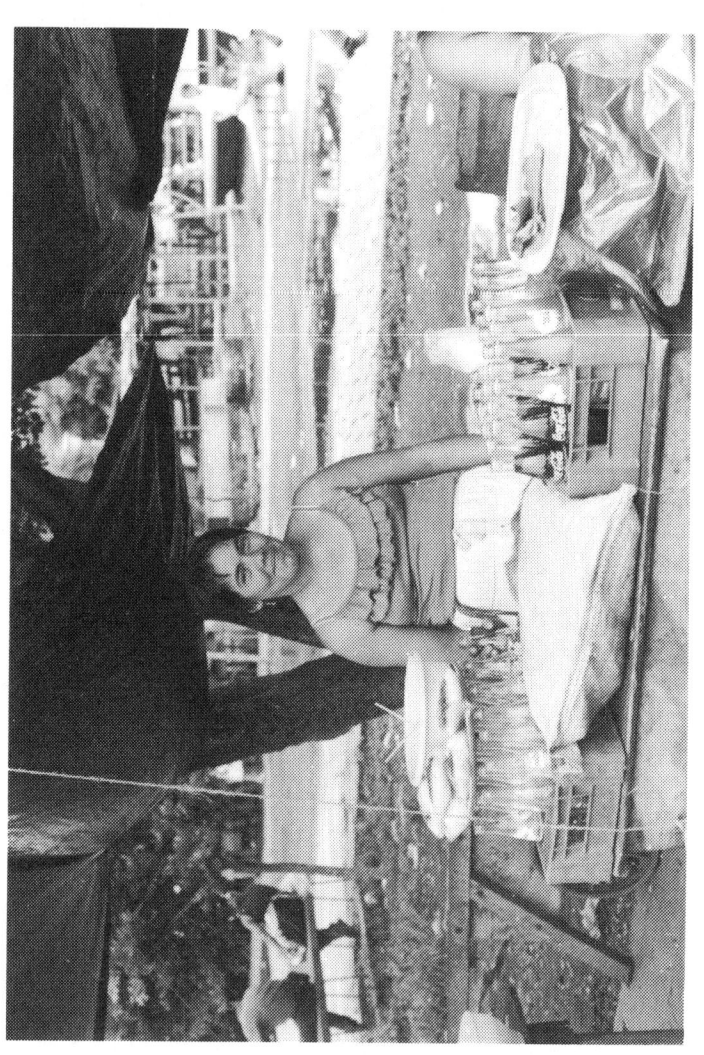

shortly after. Ten minutes later two more buses pull in, one for Managua and one for Corinto. When the driver finally opens the door the line becomes a mob which collapses on the bus, vying for the 60 or so available seats. Twenty people are trying to wedge their way through the door at the same time. Suddenly a chicken pops from the center of the struggle. An old woman fights her way out of the chaos and goes after it. She sits down on the curb and calmly puts her squawking hen back in a burlap bag. She will wait for the next bus. Two or three hours is a long time to stand.

Flora has eight Pepsis bagged and is ready to sell through the windows again. She limps around one bus and then the other. In a few minutes she returns again, this time with two bags remaining.

"It doesn't matter," she said referring to the two bags she didn't sell. "I'm going to run out today anyway."

Occasionally Flora can't get enough Coke and Pepsi to sell. This is one of those days. The pop man simply doesn't have anymore. Due to the U.S. embargo Spain and Italy have become their main suppliers, and they can't get nearly as much as they need. There are three other flavors of pop in Nicaragua: rojita (red), naranja (orange), and uva (grape). Today he has only naranja and rojita. Flora orders a case of each.

The embargo is not the only reason Coke and Pepsi are in short supply. They are also the two most popular flavors, a taste that was acquired during the forty year Somoza reign, when Nicaragua was dominated by large U.S. corporations, and Coke and Pepsi were abundant. Since then Nicaragua has slipped out of the Pepsi generation. The only "real thing" left is the war.

Three weeks later, when my plane from Managua finally arrived back in New Orleans, I was sick. I had had severe diarrhea for the last two days and the flight hadn't helped. So I was trying to find a pop machine. Seven-Up sounded good. I found a row of vending machines. Geez, things had gotten complicated since the last time I had a pop. I put in a quarter and a lighted digital readout confirmed my deposit. I added two more quarters and the readout climbed to "75." The machine started to whir.

Now I just had to decide on a flavor. Pepsi, Caffeine Free Pepsi, Diet Pepsi, Caffeine Free Diet Pepsi, Coke, Classic Coke, Caffeine Free Diet Coke, Cherry Coke, Sprite, Diet Sprite. Before I chose I checked the other machine, knowing I could get my change back. Gatorade, Slice, Diet Slice, Like, Diet Like, Country Time Lemonade, A & W Root Beer, and Diet A & W Root Beer. There was no Seven-Up on that one either! Even though there are about 100 or so brands of pop to choose from, I thought they'd have Seven-Up. They usually do. I decided on Sprite, the next best thing, and punched the square plastic logo. There was the familiar rumble of the can falling down the shoot. I reached in the door and pulled out a can of Coke.

DANNY

"You have heard that it was said, 'You shall love your neighbor and hate your enemy.' But I say to you, 'Love your enemies and pray for those who persecute you...'"
— Matthew 5:43-44

Saturday morning. The bell on the door clangs - another sweaty, impatient customer. He is well-dressed, self-assured, and wants a whole new exhaust system installed that day.

"Monday," Danny says.

The man looks surprised, frustrated, then leaves.

"Who the hell was he supposed to be?" Danny smiles, while slipping another cigarette between his lips. It rises and falls with every word as he continues.

"Everybody thinks they're the god-damned President today...must be the heat."

Danny M. manages a Midas Muffler shop in suburban Detroit. He has been, as he puts it, "running the whole show," for nearly five years. He works hard. They're open from 7:00 a.m. to 6:00 p.m., Monday through Saturday. So when Danny goes on vacation he really likes to get away. Last October he spent a month training contras at a camp in Northern Nicaragua, near the Honduran border.

"I'm not a contra though," he explains. "I love to fight. I do it for the adrenalin high."

Though he claimed he was neutral, and that the politics of the war never came up in his work, he admitted that he'd like to see the contras "pull it off."

"The money's good...sometimes. But that's not why you do it. I can make more right here selling mufflers. You do it cause you love to fight - and living on the edge. My only rule is that I will never fight for a communist unit."

He had a lot to say about communism.

"Theoretically, it's (communism) a good thing. I mean everybody shares everything and has a job and enough to eat and all that. But it never works. And it don't work because people always have a drive to get more. We always want more. You know - the American Dream and all that stuff."

I asked him how he had become a mercenary.

"If you really want to learn about this stuff go down to RECONDO (a training camp in the wilds of Alabama that specializes in two week crash courses in guerrilla warfare). You can find the address and more info in the back of Soldier of Fortune magazine. I'm going down for another session in June - to get tuned up."

He pulls down a framed color glossy from a shelf behind his desk and hands it to me. It's a picture of a soldier in a camouflaged uniform standing in the woods. He is pointing an AK-47 at the camera. There is a cigarette hanging from his mouth and a proud but unpredictable look in the small, closely set eyes. It's Danny.

"That's me last summer at RECONDO," he explains, assuming I don't recognize him.

As the day grows hotter and the customers more frequent I begin to feel like I should leave.

But Danny keeps encouraging me to stay. He seems both afraid and anxious to talk. He keeps saying, "Don't use my name" and "I can't give you any hard facts." But he never once suggests that I should leave, or seems tired of talking.

At about 12:30 a fat sweaty mechanic comes in from the garage. "O.K., we need it now."

"We gotta go for a ride," Danny tells me.

It seems 50 degrees hotter outside. We get in Danny's rusted Monte Carlo. He rolls his sleeves up and the windows down. We're going to another shop to pick up an engine. As we weave through the heavy traffic and humidity he talks more about Nicaragua.

"I was a trainer...mostly hand to hand combat and munitions operations. I worked with a group of 15 soldiers for two weeks. We lived in a lean-to or in the bush. There was nothing to eat except rice and beans and whatever we could kill, pigs or goats, even an iguana once. Most of the ones in my groups were peasants who had come to fight in exchange for food and clothes. There was an Indian too. He didn't have the slightest idea what to do with an AK-47. (Danny starts laughing). He never really learned either. I think he thought it was a damned canoe paddle."

The more Danny talked about Nicaragua the more curious I became about his Spanish proficiency. Somehow I just couldn't hear him speaking Spanish. When we arrive back at the shop I finally ask.

"Poquito," he says, and then explains. "That means a little bit."

And then, after a long pause and drag on his cigarette, "But you don't need to know much. This kind of training is better when it's non-verbal."

A few minutes later the sweaty mechanic comes in again.

"Hey, take a look at this will ya?"

"Comin'," Danny says.

I figure this is a good time to leave.

Danny gives me his card and says to write if I have any more questions.

I step out of the air conditioning and back into the oven. I stand there a minute wondering if Danny had really answered any questions. As I walk by the open door to the stop I am thinking about the Indian Danny mentioned, about how he didn't know what to do with an AK-47, and wondering why he should.

Suddenly I hear a loud repeating mechanical noise behind me. Startled, I whirl to see the fat mechanic several feet away. He is removing the lug nuts from a wheel with an air wrench. Danny is standing behind him and sees me jump. He dramatically puts both hands over his heart, as if he had just been shot.

"Did we get ya?" he asks grinning.

CHRISTMAS

"And while they were there the time came for her to be delivered. And she gave birth to her first-born son and wrapped him in swaddling clothes, and laid him in a manger, because there was no place for them in the inn."

— Luke 2:6-7

We duck in through the large glass doors, escaping yet another sub-zero blast. The suburban Chicago mall is a warm, safe myriad of red and green and tinsel. Santa Claus is taking orders in front of Penney's. Frenzied shoppers are darting between stores, trying to balance two or three awkwardly stuffed sacks and keep track of their tired, frustrated children. A muted pipe organ version of "We Three Kings" is barely distinguishable in the background. There is a sense of urgency, since it is Christmas Eve - but also a calm. It will soon all be over. No more account juggling or bickering over how much to spend on whom or worry about the escalating VISA bill.

We move through the wide polished wooden aisles, past the carefully recreated street scenes: the vintage globe lamps, park benches, and potted plants. The benches are full of exhausted shoppers, some munch on yogurt cones or caramel corn, others, with eyes closed in relief, wait for a spouse or parent or son to rescue them, to drive them home.

On our way to the escalator we pass six or seven shoe stores, four or five clothing stores, several record and book stores, a tobacco shop, a "Cookie Factory," a French bakery, and Lady Chatterly's, a new women's lingerie shop. They are all making last minute appeals to shoppers. A sign in one window reads, "Beat The Rush: After Christmas Sale Begins Today!"

The escalator is located in the center of the mall. As we ride to the second level I realize that there are many other aisles full of stores protruding in all directions, that we have seen only one aisle on one level.

Gilberto suggests we eat at McDonald's on level three. I am relieved I don't have to decide.

We get coffees, Big Macs, fries, and cherry turnovers and find a table on the edge of the main aisle. The last minute Christmas shopping fervor is whirring by us.

"Did you ever eat at the McDonald's in Managua?" Gilberto asks.

I am a little surprised by the question, but then remember that Gilberto is not a "typical" Nicaraguan. He could afford a plane ticket to flee his homeland and the Sandinista draft. He attends a major U.S. university. He speaks English and has nice clothes. His father works for the International Development Bank. Of course he'd know there was a McDonald's in Managua."

"No," I finally respond.

"We lived in Esteli, but my Dad had to go to Managua a lot," says Gilberto. "He always wanted to go to McDonald's. Under Somoza everything from the U.S. was popular - McDonald's, Pepsi, designer blue jeans. They even used to televise all the bowl games live on New Year's day. Nobody knew much about North American football, but we all watched."

He paused and took a sip of coffee and bite of his burger before continuing.

"I think they still televise 'Dynasty.' Or at least they did in '83, before I left. So that's what we saw of the U.S. - McDonald's, football, and

'Dynasty.' When I got here I realized it's a little different, that you have poverty too. But you have to look a lot harder to find it."

As we continued talking I realized that my preconception of Gilberto as a rich kid who had fled Nicaragua only so he could stay rich was a little off base. He was rich, and he did believe (like his father) that capitalism and large corporations were the answer to Nicaragua's problems. But he had also left to avoid the draft. He knew guerrilla war. He had fought with the Sandinistas against Somoza's National Guard, in both his native Esteli and later in Managua.

Gilberto had joined the Sandinistas in 1978, at 13. There were about 25 in his "battalion," a ragtag band of teenagers with a handful of .22 rifles and homemade grenades. There were a few that had had previous fighting experience, and one who was a real soldier, who had been trained in the jungle and had an AK-47.

"We fought to survive," Gilberto explained. "Somoza's Guard was burning homes and killing people indiscriminately. If they found you in the street with a bruise or scab on your arm or face they would claim you had been fighting with the Sandinistas, and would either kill you or terrorize your family. I finally joined the Sandinistas because I wanted to defend myself. But we never really knew what we were doing. We were always running. Hit a guard post and run. Hit a munition depot and run. I never felt like we won anything or made any progress. I didn't know what I was fighting for. We just kept hitting and running."

I ask him why he finally left Nicaragua then, why he abandoned his homeland, if that too wasn't a kind of running.

He is surprised at my directness and looks angry, then thoughtful. He gulps down the last of his coffee and looks me hard in the eye.

"I love my country and my people, but there's nothing there. We are barely surviving. Look at you. You go to a good college. You have a car. You have lots of food and clothes. You have malls. You have choices. I came here because I want a choice - an opportunity."

He still seems a little perturbed at me for asking such a threatening question, so I change the subject. I ask him what he'd like to do.

"After I get my Business degree I'd like to work for my Dad. He's talked about setting up an office in Miami some day. I'd be a C.P.A."

Gilberto looks with concern at his watch.

"I need to go," he says. "Uh...maybe we can talk some more later. I need to pick out a gift, pick up my wife, and get to the airport by 4:00."

They are picking up his father, who currently lives in Bogota. He is flying in to visit for the holidays.

I thank him for his time, but remain in my seat and finish my coffee. I watch perfectly groomed businessmen, frustrated housewives, slobbering and screaming babies, pink-haired teenagers with black leather boots, a stooped, tired janitor, and over-rouged, fat-layered ladies all make their way through the mall, through a world of choices.

Models of Church in Nicaragua

by Rafael Aragón & José María Vigil

MODELS OF CHURCH IN NICARAGUA

It is commonly said that the conflict in the Nicaraguan church is over political, rather than theological differences. This means that dogmatic affirmations are not what are being denied or doubted. Nonetheless, we should not believe that there are no differences in the theological positions of different Christian groups. Such differences do exist. There are different "models of church" in Nicaragua.

Furthermore, although the simplest way of presenting the conflict is a bipolar view, and although it may be very practical to classify the variations in just a few models, the reality is more complex and diverse. There are no concrete realizations of pure models but, rather, intermediate realizations and mixtures that at times defy classification. In any case, it is valuable to attempt to classify and illuminate the reality as long as we keep in mind the distance between the reality itself and any written attempt to assess it.

When we speak of "models of church," we are referring to the way the different forms of ecclesial organization and institutionalization relate to political power and to its social impact. Clearly, to talk about "models of church" is not to refer to new ways of interpreting dogma, teaching, or the life of the ecclesial community itself. The expression "models of church" refers fundamentally to the social impact of the different ecclesial manifestations that exist in Nicaragua, and to their relationship to political power.

Within this framework, we would like to describe generally the three fundamental ecclesiological models under which we can group, very roughly, the infinitely varied forms of church in Nicaragua.

These models of church are presented without discussing their historical roots. Three large schemes or configurations of the church in society are lifted up, based on the experience of the last eight years. We take for granted that reality is much richer and more dynamic and, in many cases, difficult to classify in full and rigid schemes.

Our analysis concentrates on the Roman Catholic Church. This is fundamentally the reality we wish to systematize in this study, although we will refer occasionally to Protestant churches.

1. THREE MODELS OF CHURCH

1.1. The Conservative, or Church of Christendom, Model

This is the oldest model, the one from which the others are derived. It is a common and characteristic model in the different Latin American countries that are inheritors of many centuries of colonial history.

1.1.1. Analysis of Reality

In the conservative church model – or the "church of Christendom" – the church tends not to address explicitly or critically a theme such as the analysis of reality. The church considers itself above politics, and proclaims insistently that its realm is neither politics nor temporal realities. As a moral power, it is above the political reality, although it judges and informs the latter with its guidance. The church seeks to influence governments directly, so that state institutions will support the church's teachings. The church also seeks its own spheres of action and influence, especially in education and in communications media.

This model of church always has shown itself to be reactionary toward any social and political change. It is a conservative and deeply anti-communist church. Yet it is unaware of its own political vision, which coincides with that of the dominant sectors with which it historically has identified and is normally linked. In its socio-economic analysis of reality, this church sees as natural and unquestionable the established order of traditional society, private property, the moral supremacy of the church over all of society, the social privileges afforded the church for the free exercise of its high pastoral mission, etc. Although it frequently invokes the terms "democracy," "human rights," "freedom of press and expression," etc., it links itself with the more conservative sectors.

We can include a large part of the masses who are sociologically Christians, but who do not play an important role in politics, under this model. Also included are many people who live a clear contradiction in consciousness: on the one hand they hold political opinions which are contrary to the official positions of the hierarchy while, on the other, they participate uncritically in traditional religious celebrations which are politically tendentious or even openly provoke attitudes that are contrary to the revolutionary process.

The religious sentiments of these masses are easily manipulated because of their lack of religious, as well as political, critical consciousness. The pastoral work of the Archdiocese of Managua has concentrated on this sector, promoting the most popular traditions of religiosity, its symbols, images and celebrations.

1.1.2. Theological-ecclesiological Vision

Christian salvation is seen as entirely separate from history. In fact, history, in this model of church, does not exist. Salvation is strictly spiritual and ahistorical, as well as individual. Therefore, salvation is obtained through individual moral and religious practices.

"Temporal realities" are not seen as autonomous, but always as subordinate to the church. The church seeks a hegemonic position in society, by means of ethics and morality, through ideological influence on education and a presence in the means of communication.

1.1.3. Pastoral Position

The pastoral position begins, confusingly, with the assumption that the people are already Christian and evangelized. The main instrument of the church's pastoral work is the practice of popular religiosity (and of some sacraments included within the same understanding of popular religiosity) unaccompanied by a sufficient evangelization effort.

Catechesis is fundamentally doctrinal and moral, within a framework of morality that is individual and detached from all social commitment, thus indirectly favoring an accommodation with the status quo. The dualism between religious practice and social reality is total.

Anything that does not have the approval of hierarchical authority is bad and dangerous, always viewed with distrust. Thus, the vision of ecumenism, for example, is limited exclusively to institutional relationships that have the approval of the hierarchy.

In general, pastoral work is sustained more through institutions than through Christian communities. Ecclesiastical organization is authoritarian and vertical, centralized in the bishop.

Today in Nicaragua, this model is found among a belligerent group of bishops that represent the position of the Bishops' Conference. They are surrounded by lay groups of the traditionally Catholic bourgeoisie linked to conservative political parties, including parties not represented in the National Assembly because they did not participate in the elections of November 4, 1984.

Also included in this model is a broad sector of older diocesan priests and religious – national and foreign – and a new generation of Nicaraguan priests that control the important positions in the Managua

Curia and direct or coordinate the lay movements: <u>cursillos</u>, the charismatic movement, marriage encounters, etc. These movements, although welcomed by sectors of the Christian people, are directed and encouraged mainly by the monied bourgeoisie.

1.1.4. Attitude Toward the Revolution

This model of church adopts an attitude toward the Revolution which is conservative (becoming a voice for the most conservative sectors), reactionary (refusing to open itself to any process of change), and counterrevolutionary (its proposals coincide with those of counterrevolutionary and imperialist sectors). This church tries not to recognize the legitimacy of the Revolution, its government, its laws. This model considers the Revolution to be reversible, and does not hide the fact that its greatest wish is for that possibility to become a reality. Its actions and attitudes toward reality, especially its public statements, often merge with U.S. policy and thus legitimate the latter's strategies.

The church in this model sees itself "de-throned," in that it does not hold a hegemonic, or even privileged, position in society. This church considers itself persecuted when it encounters competition or rivalry in functions which it traditionally has fulfilled exclusively; for example, when the Revolution, through its own process, becomes a source of values and moral inspiration. In this situation, the hierarchy suffers a strong identity crisis, feels displaced, and places the blame on persecution and lack of freedom. It takes advantage of opportune moments to confront the revolutionary government and to create conflicts that aggravate the situation, hoping for a way out and a change in the situation. The conflict is always dressed in pastoral clothing, although it may be purely political.

The people, sociologically religious and lacking catechetical preparation, are confused. This confusion frequently manifests itself by participation in traditional religious practice which is in clear contradiction to the peoples' political commitment A great imbalance often can be observed between the peoples' advanced political consciousness and their participation in religious celebrations that are charged with traditional ideology and counterrevolutionary political subtleties. When a person experiences the conflict between his/her political option and his/her traditional religious practice, s/he may come to reject the practice, fall into a state of indifference, or even adopt aggressive attitudes toward all religious practice, especially if, in moments of crisis, the church has not accompanied the person with an adequate pastoral posture for the new situation.

1.2. The Renewal Model

The emergence of this model is closely related to the developmental process of the 1960's in Latin America, and to the biblical, liturgical, and ecumenical renewal that culminated in the process that led to the Second Vatican Council.

1.2.1. Analysis of Reality

In this model, unlike the previous one, the church opens its eyes to societal problems but sees no need to adopt solutions involving structural change. Rather, this church promotes change in moral attitudes, together with aid to development. Faced with poverty, under-development, misery, etc., this church does not try to change structures but, rather, people, so that they will be good, and so that society will function better and avoid these lamentable situations. The system is not bad; it just, naturally enough, has failings that need to be corrected. This model's analysis of reality is classically called "functionalist." Development is seen as a linear historical process, without ruptures, based on the directions put forth in the developed countries of the first world.

1.2.2. Theological-ecclesiological Vision

In this model, the church emphasizes conversion of the heart and personal change, more than social aspects or structural change.

Unlike the conservative model, which bases its pastoral action on popular religiosity without evangelization, the renewal model offers an evangelization process that leads to a morality of individualistic attitudes and to community participation in the sacraments and in all of church life. It is truly a process of renewal: liturgical renewal, biblical catechesis, renewal of preaching, the appearance of new religious movements, insistence on the community aspect. However, this renewal is still situated firmly within the church. Exegetical and scientific discoveries enrich the biblical vision, the liturgy is translated and beautified, theology adopts new philosophies (personalism, existentialism) and even uses anthropology and psychology. This renewal corresponds to the ecclesiological model that emerged from the Second Vatican Council in response to the challenges that Christians face in the developed world, and to the new philosophical currents of first world culture. This church neither represents the reality of third world peoples nor responds to their problems. At the level of the world-wide church, this model corresponds to what has been called "conciliar renewal," which takes its paradigms from the European first world.

This model rediscovers salvation history, which becomes a fundamental dimension of its theoretical vision of renewal. But it always maintains that there are two histories, not to be confused with one another.

This model of church overcomes the attitude of confrontation with modern culture, and talks of going into the world in a spirit of dialogue (Gaudium et Spes). But the church's dialogue partner is the first world, the world of atheism and modernity. The third world and the world of poverty and oppression are still not considered.

Therefore, the prophetic mission of the church is not discovered. The community dimension of faith is much more emphasized. All Christian thought is re-read as salvation history, and as personalist, and existentialist. Despite the dialogue with the world, the church still maintains an ecclesiocentric position.

1.2.3. Pastoral Position

The fundamental pastoral instrument is a renewed catechesis that leads to sacramental practice, all within a conciliar community spirit. Popular religiosity is abandoned to some degree, since it is considered a primitive form that must give way to the new religious practices renewed by the Second Vatican Council.

This model sees pastoral work as the proper realm of the church. The political has nothing to do with what is specifically pastoral. Political work is a specific task of the laity. While it is true that the Conciliar documents offer a more advanced perspective, this stance is represented in the pastoral and political attitudes maintained by "the official church" in the reality of pastoral practice. The laity must commit itself to projects of Christian inspiration.

In fact, in this model, pastoral action and the life of the church are free of their political dimension. The most commonly used themes are human rights, freedom of expression, of thought, of conscience (Pacem in Teris), without ever entering into the socio-structural dimension: justice, causes of poverty and underdevelopment, etc. The church's functionalist vision of society understands underdevelopment as a phenomenon of social, political, economic, and cultural backwardness, and sees the solution to these problems in a process of development within the capitalist system itself, without ruptures or structural changes. This church favors development projects, in which it participates on good terms with governments, and receiving in exchange governmental cooperation in efforts to overcome social evils – thus providing the church with a precious social space for its actions. With these kinds of projects and social participation, the church becomes an important legitimator of the system, identifying itself with the progressive and modernist bourgeois classes.

Therefore, the church does not enter explicitly into the area of politics. But it does enter the social sphere, understood without radicalism, along the lines of the Populorum Progressio. The church finds a great pastoral platform through its charitable works, its "own works." Through them, the church fulfills an obligation of the state, responding to needs that the government is not resolving and thus bringing about good understanding between church and state. A reciprocal movement is created: covering for the state, the church legitimates the latter's social policies. And the state gives the church favors and privileges, allowing it to carry out its "own works" (schools, hospitals, means of communication, aid for worship and clergy) thus helping the church to have a place in society, a visible presence, moral influence, pastoral platforms, etc.

1.2.4. Attitude Toward the Revolution

Before the triumph of the Revolution, this model of church did not relate to popular movements because their politics did not fall within the system. As long as possible, the church ignored the popular movements. When their emergence made it impossible to ignore them, the church initially confronted them on issues of violence, human rights, property, atheism, materialism and anti-communism. When the popular movements began to use violence, the church hierarchy, who up to that point had never spoken out about institutionalized violence, began to speak of its rejection of violence "from wherever it may come." It adopted a supposedly neutral position, with one message for the dominant sectors of society (basically a call to moderation, reform, aid to development, the social duties of private property, etc.) and another for the emerging popular movement (rejection of violence, historical patience, recognition of private property, the danger of materialism and atheism in Marxist ideologies, etc.).

This model of church experienced extensive growth before the triumph of the Revolution, enlivened by groups of organized and committed Christians in ecclesial base communities, by youth groups, and by priests and religious who were more open in their pastoral work. Progressive pastoral work played an important role in public opinion and in calling together the masses of Christian people, opening broad spaces for collaboration and participation in the revolutionary process and the insurrection.

After the triumph of the Revolution, the consequences of the ideological conflict throughout the church began to appear. Broad sectors from this model of the church leaned toward the revolutionary process. Others joined the conservative tendency of the traditional sectors of the hierarchy. Yet another group more or less abstained from political conflict, carrying out its social projects in a relationship of respectful understanding with the government.

1.3. Liberating Model

This model emerged in Nicaragua around a pastoral experience during 1966, in courses for Delegates of the Word in the parish of St. Paul the Apostle and the eastern areas of Managua; in the experience of

Gaspar Garcia Laviana and the Rural Pastoral Team; in the experience of Solentiname; in the young people's community of Barrio Riguero, and the different experiences of religious women involved in CONFER (the national conference of women religious).

1.3.1. Analysis of Reality

This model of church emerged in the moment when development theory was being replaced by dependency theory. It adopted a dialectical analysis of reality. Underdevelopment was interpreted according to the new theories of Latin American social sciences. Underdevelopment was no longer thought of as simply backwardness with respect to capitalism, but rather as its consequence, that is, as dependent capitalism.

This analysis comes out of the reality and social location of the poor. This church removes itself from the dominant classes' framework of reality in the secular world to be the only objective view of reality. This church makes its own conscious and reflective analysis of reality. It is aware of ideological interventions, and adopts a critical position toward them. It discovers the structural character of injustice and social conflict. It makes an option for the poor. It opts for overcoming capitalism, for a radical change of the system. It supports the popular cause and its organized movement.

1.3.2. Theological-ecclesiological Vision

This model's theological vision is marked by the rediscovery of Jesus: the historical Jesus, his cause, his announcement of the Realm of the Good News for the Poor, of God the Creator of all who wish to live as brothers and sisters and commit themselves historically with the people to build a new, fraternal world.

An incarnated and historical reading of faith and the Bible is undertaken. Injustice and poverty are discovered to be structural sin, justice to be the practice of love, evangelization to be a process of conscientization, theology to be critical reflection on the praxis of faith, the social sciences (rather than philosophy) to be the new theological intervention, and history – and history alone – to be the place where Christian salvation is realized while moving toward the eschatological moment.

This analysis of reality leads to discovering the impossibility of neutrality or a supposed apolitical stance. It is therefore conscious of the political implication of faith.

At the ecclesiological level, the church is conceived as the pilgrim people of God in history, as the people, the base. The role of the laity, more democratic management of the church, lay ministry, participation, and more equal and fraternal relations are all emphasized.

Ecclesiocentrism is overcome when the Realm of God is discovered as an absolute theme. The church is not the Realm, but must put itself at the service of the Realm, and must feel itself permanently being converted toward the Realm. Nor is the church the only possible locus of the Realm; rather the Kingdom is present in many other human realities, thus requiring the church to have a much more broadly ecumenical approach. The church must not put the world at its service, but should put itself at the service of building the Realm in this world. Therefore, the church must become incarnate in the world like Jesus, and must enter into the world of the poor, also like Jesus.

The church must proclaim the Good News for the poor that Jesus announced. It must make the option for the poor that Jesus made, from the social location of the poor, carrying the option to its final consequences and, like Jesus, accepting the consequences of the conflicts it unleashes. The church must assume the prophetic, critical and martyrial function that propelled Jesus.

The ecclesial base communities emerge as the institutional expression (the visible charisma) of the faith experience of the poor. This is why the base communities are part of the popular movement. They are a new way of being church and from this perspective, they question the whole church.

1.3.3. Pastoral Position

Pastoral work begins with reality and concrete necessities. It integrates evangelization and human promotion, evangelization and conscientization, liberation and salvation. It accentuates the community character of faith and the community's commitment to the social and political process. The political implications of pastoral work are accepted. The methodology of popular education is adopted.

The option for the poor is concretized in the option for the popular classes, living among them and unleashing an "Exodus process" and sharing it with them. This causes a profound change in many pastoral agents. The church is living the same history as the popular movement, and so lives in an hour of martyrdom. It has a positive relationship with the popular movements, and a conflictive one with anti-popular governments. The church values its evangelizing and prophetic function more than its sacramental or doctrinal role, and favors orthopraxis over orthodoxy.

2. THREE MODELS IN NICARAGUA

The most reactionary sector of the clergy and some bishops are found within the conservative model of church. Not all the clergy, however, would subscribe to this model.

Although it is clear that the Second Vatican Council did not have deep repercussions in the Nicaraguan church's pastoral work, it did open a road for renewal among a group of young priests who were concerned about pastoral renewal in Nicaragua, and especially about giving pastoral attention to an emerging generation of youth with a clear political consciousness. This new generation of priests, later supported by the new impact on the Nicaraguan church of the documents and conclusions of the Second Conference of Latin American Bishops in Medellin, Colombia, injected broad sectors with the energy of renewal that characterized church life from 1968 to 1979. In recent years, then, it is not so much a question of no advance in the revolution and renewal of the church in Nicaragua, but of a backward movement toward forms, uses, plans, and practices that had been surpassed and abandoned in the period of conciliar renewal.

Also included in this model are conservative movements like that of Kiko Arguello (wrongly called the "catechumens") and others like it. Although these were born out of a renewal and conciliar model of church, they have, in recent years, been coopted by the more conservative sectors and introduced into the conservative model, doing violence to their own original designs.

Conservative political groups enter fully into this model of church, and now appear with a religious fervor that never characterized them before, this sector of the church and hierarchy having become the conservatives' best ally and principal spokesperson.

A clear expression of backward movement, as noted above, can be seen in the emphasis on a popular religiosity that was devalued and somewhat unnoticed in the time of Conciliar renewal, and which has been revived in recent years with explicitly conservative and preconciliar pastoral aims. (Examples are: the appearances at Cuapa, the "kidnapping" of the Blood of Christ, the reinitiation of practices that had disappeared, pilgrimages to the most traditional sanctuaries.)

What we have called the "renewal model" of church never crystallized in Nicaragua to any significant degree. A broad sector of the Nicaraguan clergy which had assimilated deeply the Conciliar renewal and given themselves to it, could have been identified within this model. However, the ideological confrontation within the Nicaraguan church radicalized positions and limited the space for dialogue with the Revolution. Thus, pressures from Rome and from the Bishops' Conference dissolved the Association of Nicaraguan Clergy, ACLEN, which had followed this line of thought. Some sectors of clergy that were very linked to ACLEN, but who were marginalized because of the conflict, are working effectively in parishes of the Granada and Esteli Diocese.

This model could also apply to a significant sector of Protestant churches, very much tied to international agencies of the First World, that became organized after the 1972 earthquake in Managua to carry out projects of aid and development. On the Atlantic Coast, a broad sector of Cappuchin priests, religious and lay pastoral workers, and the pastoral work as a whole, supported by the bishops, could be included in the renewal model, along with other broad sectors led by more progressive Nicaraguan and foreign priests.

Within the liberating model of church we find, above all, the experiences of the base communities the Delegates of the Word. These were originally born within the renewal model, later to discover the arena of social action and finally the meaning of revolutionary politics. The communities have experienced the same contradiction as the rest of the Nicaraguan church. Some arose among popular organizations and peasant unions; others have been controlled and directed by hierarchical pressures toward the more conservative church. In any case, broad sectors in the northern part of the country, in Somotillo and Esteli, and numerous groups continue to work along the line of the liberating model. There are also cases on the Atlantic Coast of pastoral work that fit within this model.

The so-called "centers" of theological reflection and social development, some instances of youth work, groups of revolutionary bourgeois and revolutionary Christians who work in the government fit within this model. Finally, the whole effort at better coordination of the Church of the Poor is part of this model. This effort is manifested by the "evangelical insurrection," initiated by Miguel D'Escoto's fast and, later, the Procession to the Stations of the Cross for Peace and Life; and it is strengthened by the presence of numerous religious and new lay pastoral agents who have incorporated themselves into pastoral work in recent years, especially in the newer areas of Managua and in the peasant zones most affected by the war.

Models of the Church

	Conservative Model	Renewal Model	Liberating Model
Church	Perfect Society Hierarchy Institution	People of God Summoned community which celebrates movements and groups.	At the service of the Realm of the organized people. Ecclesial Base Communities Network of CEBs and ministries
Relation with the world	The world at the service of the church.	Dialogue with the world.	Inserted in the world to construct the Realm of God.
Politics	Politics at the service of the church. The church is naively apolitical.	Pastoral political autonomy. Church seeks to be apolitical.	Christians involved in politics. Church consciously political.
History	History does not exist.	Secular history and salvation history.	One history only.
Christology	Christ the King	The titles of Jesus.	Jesus Christ the liberator.
Maryology	Most Blessed Virgen	Mother of the Church	Mary of Nazareth, mother of Jesus.
Spiritual Life	Ascetic and mystical.	Personal conversion.	New person and new world.
Utopia	Eternal salvation	The banquet of the Realm of Heaven as the fullness of grace.	The Realm of God.
Social place	Power, higher stratum	Reformist bourgeoisie and middle classes.	The popular subject. The poor.
Liturgy	Religious practices	Sacramental liturgy in the faith community.	Celebration of community life and history.
Pastoral mediation	Religious practices	Evangelization for the sacraments.	Transforming praxis, construction of the Realm.
Theology	Explanations from the magesterium, defined by the magesterium.	Culturalist theology taken from the biblical renewal, patristics, etc.	Critical reflection regarding the practice of faith based on reality.
Auxiliary Sciences	Scholasticism	Personalism, existentialism, anthropology, psychology	Social sciences
Ecumenicity	Anything non-Catholic is perverse.	Dialogue with "seperated brethen."	United in the cause of the poor for the construction of the Realm of God.

3. ECCLESIAL BASE COMMUNITIES AND THE POST-REVOLUTIONARY ECCLESIOLOGICAL MODEL

Of particular interest is the route followed in recent years by the popular masses - above and beyond the more conscious popular groups that have been involved in base communities since the 1970's. For a long time the popular masses remained anchored in the conservative model, identified as Christian mainly by the practice of popular religiosity. Conciliar renewal did not exercise much influence on them. However, the 1969 Pastoral Assembly, the presence of the base communities, the priests' movements, plus youth work and the Catholic school movement, served to create favorable public opinion toward the participation of Christians in the Revolution. Carlos Mejia Godoy and his musical group "Gradas," the Permanent Commission on Human Rights (which included Fathers Fernando Cardenal and Edgar Parrales, both of whom left their posts after the triumph of the Revolution to become part of the government's cabinet), Father Uriel Molina (who also withdrew to found the Antonio Valdivieso Ecumenical Center), the radio schools of the Cappuchin fathers, Radio Catolica in its better time, Gaspar Garcia Laviana, the critical posture that Obando finally adopted toward the dictatorship, the role played by the church in the most difficult moments as a space to bring people together against the dictatorship (for example, the "journalism of the catacombs") - all of these converged definitively to affect popular religiosity, making it the vanguard for the more conscious groups within the Church of the Poor.

Thus, the majority of the people passed directly from the conservative model to revolutionary participation. This incorporation of the masses into the Revolution took place with no contradiction to their faith, but also without a truly revolutionary consciousness, mature on the political, as well as the religious, level. This explains the conflict and confusion among a broad sector of Christians after the enthusiasm of the revolutionary triumph had passed.

After the 1972 earthquake in Managua, the political confrontation deepened and Christians continually had to confront the challenges of political action. These were the years when Christians encountered each other in popular and revolutionary processes at all organizational levels. The base communities were deeply involved in this integration into political militancy. Within the church, the communities assumed a position of critical and political belligerence against the dictatorship, thus accompanying the process of the people.

This integration limited direct pastoral action, especially the formation of new pastoral agents and the incorporation of new members. Prophetic action and political commitment absorbed the community's life. With the triumph of the Revolution, Christians thus involved entered fully into the revolutionary process, and the best leaders became part of the leadership in popular organizations. Many died along the way.

On the other hand, since the triumph of the Revolution, the base communities have ceased being the only possible sphere of political struggle. The new sphere has become the Revolution itself, the sphere won by the people as the subjects of their own history. The ecclesial base communities, no longer the point of convocation and encounter for social struggle, entered into a period of crisis over their social identity.

Furthermore, the Revolution, as a human experience, became a total experience: the source of values, meaning, utopia, tasks, generosity, morale, etc. Thus the Revolution fulfilled for many the need for meaning and values that previously was satisfied only by the Christian community and the church as a religious reference. This has caused the hierarchy - as noted above - to feel surpassed or replaced in its function, and also caused the Christian base community to lose the convoking power that it had in pre-insurrectionary times.

We must add that the new subject of power is the people, because of explicit consciousness. Christians become very jealous when faced with the possibility that the "church's own works" might be duplicated by what must be effected by the new popular historical subject. More than a few ecclesial instances were invaded with a crisis of identity and meaning. Thus, in the revolutionary fervor of the first months, there was no dearth of pastoral agents who thought - precipitously - that they had discovered that the base communities could be subsumed by the Sandinista Defense Committees.

So there is no doubt whatsoever that the new social situation brought by the Revolution implies a crisis within the very structural configuration of a model of church in a given social situation. Not in vain does the Revolution mean a qualitative change, nor in vain is the church called to incarnate that change in its own time.

It is on this reality that we reflect.

The ecclesial base communities were born in the popular movement as an institutional expression of the church. In pre-revolutionary times, there was a convergence between the popular movement and the ecclesial movement. When the Revolution triumphed, there was a transfer of interests from the community to the Revolution. The base community is no longer necessary for organizing, since the people are now the historical subject of the new society and have their own organizations.

The "founding members" of the base communities in the 1960's formed them out of their profound religious experience in a process of personal conversion, related initially to the model of Conciliar renewal, out of which they later discovered social action and political commitment. Their pastoral work out was mostly centered on the ideological struggle in Nicaragua, in the fruit of the manipulation that sectors opposed to the revolutionary process made of the religious message, of its traditional symbols, of the Pope and of ecclesiastical authority. On more than one occasion these conflicts have absorbed the life of the church community, forcing it to leave to one side the work of pastoral accompaniment and formation of new members. Conflicts with the hierarchy have led the base communities to struggle more for their ecclesial legitimacy than for the implementation of a pastoral plan of growth and of pastoral accompaniment, especially during the first years.

All the factors noted can explain the decline of base communities in the revolutionary situation (since the triumph) in Nicaragua. The enormous effort undertaken in recent years to reorganize and revitalize them has not shown the fruits that might be expected. This should not be interpreted as a failure, but rather as an indication that perhaps a different path is needed. We are in a new stage of presence and of action, which we must discover with creativity and discernment under the impulse of the Spirit. This is our challenge.

There are other experiences with which we are not sufficiently familiar to discuss in this essay: for example, the base communities in the barrios of Esteli.

Currently in the cities there are not, in fact, many dynamic and creative base communities, but only a few groups or the remains of groups. The new groups that have emerged in new barrios, with the participation of pastoral agents incorporated since the triumph, center their work more on traditional functions (celebration of the Sunday Eucharist, catechesis, formation of small Bible study groups, etc.). They seek to create a better process of integrating faith and its traditional celebrations with reality, hoping to form new communities in the poorest areas of Managua. There are scarcely any base communities that bring together men and women who live out their faith within the revolutionary process, who have an organized revolutionary militancy along with a deep and dynamic religious dimension which brings them together to see and review their commitment in light of their faith. What we see, rather, are groups of women and men who come together out of traditional religious feeling, and who accept the Revolution. But when they take on tasks or positions of responsibility in popular organizations, they stay away from specifically pastoral commitment and are absent from community meetings.

Why?

It would be interesting to venture - only to "venture," while awaiting new judgments and information - some responses to this question. Perhaps the atmosphere of the base communities no longer responds to the new needs of a revolutionary society. Perhaps we have not found a new methodology for the base communities in the revolutionary situation. Perhaps we have not found the right way to locate Christian experience within that "totalizing" - all-encompassing - experience that the Revolution represents for many people. Perhaps the consequences of the mistakes and negligence of our previous pastoral work, mentioned above, are affecting us more than we thought. Perhaps the Revolution accelerates a process of secularization. We also must take into account human weakness and error, fatigue, loss of a sense of belonging, etc. In any case, the use that the Catholic hierarchy has made of its institutional authority has weighed heavily - an overwhelming weight for many simple people - in a confrontation with the liberating model of church. This role of the hierarchy disconcerts and blocks many people. Many, given the conflictive situation, prefer to privatize their Christianity, to avoid more difficulties in a Nicaraguan society already burdened with enough difficulties. Perhaps the scandal of a Catholic hierarchy that neither supports the people nor denounces the aggression it suffers has caused many to lose faith in the church, especially young people and revolutionaries. Perhaps certain Marxist dogmatisms effect some intermediate cadre and young people returning from study abroad.

Perhaps the greatest challenge now consists in knowing how to accompany so many militants who, since the triumph of the Revolution, have not found a place in the church or the base community because they are absorbed in their revolutionary tasks, or because they feel uncomfortable in the base community setting, or because of the scandal of the church. The important thing is not to try and reproduce the exact model of what base communities formerly have been within the liberating model of the church.

It can be said that, in some measure, revolutionary Nicaragua is also an ecclesiological laboratory where, in the face of incredibly urgent challenges, the church is seeking new formulas to go along with the circumstances, formulas that still have not been found. The Church of the Poor in Nicaragua is plowing new ground, attempting new models with no models to copy, and doing all this in conditions which are most unfavorable to conducting such an ecclesiological experiment in peace and serenity.

In any case, in conclusion, it should be pointed out: we do not have a definitive model to express the experience of Christians within this process, experience that goes beyond that of the Christian groups and communities that existed before the triumph of the Revolution. The people, the majority of whom are believers, participated in the insurrection and joined in all plans and organizations of the process after the triumph without finding conflicts between their faith and their political practice. This Christian people has not had a pastoral accompaniment adequate for the new situation and for their political commitment. Moreover, it has experienced intensely the ideological conflict and pastoral abandonment by bishops and priests.

In the Church of the Poor in Nicaragua, there is an incontestable and legitimate revolutionary Christian experience. In the first months of the Revolution it was thought that this experience would permeate the entire Nicaraguan church. This hope was frustrated, certainly, and its frustration was led by the hierarchy. But even without the widespread support of the church, the legitimate and incontestable testimony of the Church of the Poor in Nicaragua is still alive.

The Nicaraguan revolutionary project makes possible the participation of Christians in the Revolution. This is one of the essential characteristics maintained by the Revolution, faithful to its principles and origins, in spite of the fact that many - and, lamentably, not a few Christians - wish the opposite were the case.

At this time, the most important thing is for the Church of the Poor to be a witness to the church's prophetic presence in the midst of the revolutionary process, creating spaces for encounter and celebration, gatherings and reflections in the light of faith. It must be present at the decisive moments of life, death, mobilization of young people, etc., with a posture of pastoral accompaniment. It must create spaces of "symbolic reference" for the believing and revolutionary people. The Christian and revolutionary people must feel "affectively" accompanied by priests, pastors, communities. Above all, the Church of the Poor must be present in the process of forming the new Nicaraguan consciousness in its new cultural expressions, in the new ideology, contributing its experience and the witness of evangelical and Christian values.

PUBLICATIONS AVAILABLE FROM
NEW YORK CIRCUS PUBLICATIONS, INC.

KAIROS: Central America: A Challenge to the Churches of the World. A Document signed by more than one hundred Central American Churchleaders. 1988. $5.00.

The Church Born by God's Power in Central America: An Essay on the Popular Church. Pablo Richard, 1985. $4.95.

The Voice of a People in Struggle: The Life of Fr. Rafael Maroto. Jorge Naravez, 1986. With a special introduction on the Chilean Popular Church by Pablo Richard. $6.95.

The Neoconservative Offensive: U.S. Churches and the Ideological Struggle for Latin America. Ana Maria Ezcurra, 1983. With special introductions by Michael McIntyre and Cornel West. $4.95.

Ideological Agression Against the Sandinista Revolution: The Political Opposition Church in Nicaragua. Ana Maria Ezcurra, 1984. With special introductions by Pablo Richard and David J. Kalke. $6.95.

The Reagan Administration and the Vatican: Convergences in Central America. Ana Maria Ezcurra, 1986. With special introductions by Wayne Barrett, Pablo Richard and David J. Kalke. $6.95.

Evangelization and Politics: Addresses and Papers from an Internal Conference of Theologians at the Evangelical Seminary, Matanzas, Cuba. Edited by Sergio Arce and Oden Marichal, 1982. $4.95.

The Church and Socialism: Reflections from a Cuban Context. Sergio Arce, 1985. $6.95.

Seeds of a People's Church: Challenge and Promise from the Underside of History. Linda Unger and Kathleen Schultz, 1981. $4.50.

Available from the New York CIRCUS, Inc.
P. O. Box 37
Times Square Station
New York, NY   10108

amanecer

ENGLISH EDITION

CHRISTIAN REFLECTION IN THE NEW NICARAGUA

AMANECER IN ENGLISH offers the English-speaking world the first systematically prepared and distributed information and reflection from the Christian experience in the new Nicaragua.

$20 per year for individuals
$35 per year for institutions
(foreign subscribers add $5.00)

P.O. Box 681
Audubon Station
New York, NY 10032

DATE DUE

FEB ? '90			
MAY 2 '90			
APR 10 '91			
DEC 2 '91			
JAN 31 1995			

HIGHSMITH #LO-45220